THE AMERICAN
UNITY & INTEGRITY PROJECT

Series #1 of The American Unity and Integrity Project
WIN has published three essential books for those who take the threat of authoritarianism seriously.

The Cost of Doing Nothing Is a Price We Cannot Pay
Rabbi Henry Jay Karp

Rabbi Karp explains the reasons he believes it is appropriate to compare 1930-1940s Nazi Germany with American politics today. He details the strategy Adolf Hitler described in his book, *Mein Kampf,* and compares it to the steps President Trump uses today. We must not underestimate the determination of those who want ultimate power.

You Are Not Alone:
Your Roadmap to Effective Political Action
Gary Lucks, JD

Political activist Gary Lucks provides a guide for anyone who feels discouraged, anxious, or powerless in the face of today's political chaos. Instead of watching from the sidelines, Gary shows you how to step into meaningful action. You will be introduced to a nationwide movement of citizens committed to protecting democracy and resisting authoritarian threats. Along the way, you'll find practical tools for getting involved, stories of grassroots success, and the reassurance that you are not in this fight by yourself.

The American Oath Project:
Protecting the Backbone of Democracy
Kevin K. Johnson, MA, JD

The American Oath Project was created by experienced mediator and California civil trial and appellate lawyer Kevin K. Johnson, JD, and seeks to educate, unify, and empower the American people to take legal and civic action, guided by the spirit and principles of the United States Constitution. The book proposes the pursuit of civil lawsuits designed to end Mr. Trump's Presidential Employment Contract for both premeditated and ongoing, cumulative and coordinated breaches of the Presidential Oath of Office, and for committing "fraud in the inducement" by lying when he took the Oath.

★ ★ ★ ★ ★

GOING ON OFFENSE

THE AMERICAN OATH PROJECT

Protecting the Backbone of Democracy

KEVIN K. JOHNSON
Attorney & Mediator

The American Oath Project
Protecting the Backbone of Democracy
Copyright © 2025 by Kevin K. Johnson

All rights reserved. No part of this publication, whether in print or electronic format, may be reproduced, stored in a retrieval system, or transmitted in any form or by any means, electronic, mechanical, photocopying, recording, or otherwise, without the prior written permission of the publisher except for use of quotations in a book review.

This book represents the personal views and opinions of the author and does not necessarily reflect the positions or opinions of any organization, institution, or individual with which the author is affiliated. The content presented herein is based on the author's perspective and interpretation of the subject matter. Neither the publisher nor any associated parties shall be held responsible for any consequences arising from the opinions or interpretations expressed within this book.

First paperback edition November 2025

Published by Writers Integrity Network
Glendora, California

www.writersintegritynetwork.com
ISBN: (Paperback) 979-8-9987743-4-8

Praise for *The American Oath Project*

We simply must do everything possible to save our country and our democracy. *The American Oath Project* should be a cornerstone of that effort. If you pledge to support and defend the Constitution, then you should be held accountable when you fail to meet that contractual obligation. The rule of law is an absolute necessity for a healthy democratic republic.

—Winston Hickox, Principle, California Strategies
Former Secretary of the California
Environmental Protection Agency

Kevin Johnson's book, *The American Oath Project*, is one of the most important and well-documented projects that I have seen. There can be no doubt that extra attention needs to be paid to an administration that is out of control, and which even the Supreme Court seems reluctant to remedy. How such a legal action could proceed will be up to those who would litigate it, but it seems clear that a prima facie case has been made.

—Oliver Houck, Emeritus Professor and
David Boies Chair in Public Interest Law
Tulane University, New Orleans, Louisiana

President Trump unleashed Project 2025 which has kept NGOs and state attorneys general on the defensive in the face of unrelenting lawlessness and attacks on the Constitution and democratic institutions. *The American Oath Project* flips the script offering a sharp and proactive offensive litigation strategy to defend the rule of law and put the Trump regime on its heels.

—Gary A. Lucks CPEA JD, author of
You Are Not Alone: Your Roadmap to Effective Political Action, adjunct professor,
and political policy advisor

Contents

Introduction ix
Chapter 1 - A Profound and Abiding
             Debt of Gratitude... 1
Chapter 2 - Where Impeachment is not an Option 9
Chapter 3 - Breach of the Presidential Oath of Office
             and the Faithful Execution Clause 29
Chapter 4 - Conspiratorial Bad Actors, Pardons
             and Emoluments 41
Chapter 5 - Presidential Immunity, Standing to
             Sue, and Public Advocacy 49
Chapter 6 - Actively Supporting the Federal
             Courts 59
Chapter 7 - Supporting Our Military Through
             our Veterans.. 73
Chapter 8 - Educating the Voters and Using The
             News Cycle 79
Chapter 9 - Parallel State Actions 83
Chapter 10 - A Symbol for A Mass Movement............. 95
Chapter 11 - Educating Ourselves and Joining
             Together 105
Afterword 109
Table Of Authorities.. 111
Appendices... 119
Acknowledgments... 183
About the Author 185

Dedication

This book is dedicated to all the Americans over the last
238 years who have taken, in good faith,
an Oath to uphold the United States Constitution, the
"Backbone of Democracy."

Introduction

This book proposes the pursuit of civil lawsuits designed to end Mr. Trump's Presidential Employment Contract for both premeditated and ongoing, cumulative and coordinated breaches of the Presidential Oath of Office, and for committing "fraud in the inducement" by lying when he took the Oath.

The proposed actions are a central feature of the American Oath Project, which seeks to educate, unify, and empower the American people to legal and civic action, guided by the spirit and principles of the United States Constitution.

Our country's foundational governing document was wisely and compassionately crafted to evolve, adapt, and reasonably keep pace with advances in human knowledge, science, and society. It was brilliantly designed to be a "living, breathing document" that could be interpreted by future generations to effectuate the following Preamble goals:

> "We the People of the United States, in order to form a more perfect union, establish justice, insure domestic tranquility, provide for the common defense, promote the general welfare, and secure the blessings of liberty to ourselves and our posterity, do ordain and establish this Constitution for the United States of America."

Our Founders set up a "democratic republic" that combined principles of both representative democracy and direct (majority-rule) democracy, prioritizing the rights of citizens over those of the government. Over the last 238 years, millions of Americans have taken an oath to uphold the Constitution. It is time to breathe new life into this remarkable gift by reasonably interpreting and applying its express terms, its collective spirit, and centuries of related contract case law (aka "common law"), to "Show Mr. Trump the White House Door."

In taking the oath, Mr. Trump swore to "faithfully execute the Office of the President of the United States," and to the best of his ability, to "preserve, protect and defend the Constitution ..." In doing so, he also committed to "take care" that the laws of the country be "faithfully executed" by all those in the executive branch.

The oath was an express prerequisite to exercising the powers of the Presidency, and upon taking it, he became a full employee of the U.S. Government with an employment contract—the Constitution.

The sworn commitment to faithful execution imposed three duties: not to act beyond the scope of powers granted to the executive, not to use the office to enrich himself, and to perform all of his duties diligently, honestly, and in good faith.

By repeatedly violating each of these duties, Mr. Trump has materially breached his employment contract and continues to breach the contract in his relentless pursuit of a wide-ranging, completely unprecedented, and written plan to dismantle our democratic republic; to seize authoritarian, unilateral control of the country; and to intimidate and/or punish all opposition. (See "A Partial List of Oath/Contract Breaches" on p.18)

Material breaches of a contract give rise, under long-established legal authority, including common law, to the remedy of rescission of the contract. Rescission is the act of abrogating, annulling, or vacating. By committing fraud in the inducement when Mr. Trump took the

Presidential Oath, a court could declare the Presidential Contract "void," meaning it never went into effect.

These remedies, while not used before with a U.S. president, logically exist alongside the express remedy of impeachment, as the Founders never intended that we would be helpless to stop a ruthless authoritarian when circumstances made impeachment impossible. As one law professor has written, the Constitution is not to be interpreted as a "Suicide Pact" in which there is no perceived remedy for an egregious wrong.

Further, the Founders intended that centuries of common law precedent and equitable remedies could be used in conjunction with a fair and balanced reading of the Constitution to meaningfully address specific circumstances they did not draft for nor anticipate.

The Constitution is fundamentally a contract between the states and the federal government, for the benefit of the contracting parties and primarily for We the People. It was intended to be interpreted and applied in the future to implement the parties' basic intents and goals as articulated in the preamble.

A careful, unemotional evaluation of the voting history of the current members of the Supreme Court and the various pressures, fears, values, and emotions that the Justices are living with today, suggest the possibility of a majority voting to find a material breach of the employment contract and to issue an order that the contract be rescinded or that as a result of committing fraud in taking the oath, the contract never went into effect because it was void at the outset.

Win, lose, or draw, we owe it to our ancestors, our children, our grandchildren, and future generations to stand up for how the Constitution should be respected, interpreted, and applied, and insist that Mr. Trump be held accountable for his ongoing unlawful conduct, starting when he fraudulently took the Oath of Office.

Win, lose, or draw, we need to collectively and peacefully stand together, with all those who have taken, in good faith, an oath to uphold the Constitution, including active-duty and military veterans, civil servants, the judiciary, and members of law enforcement. We need to honor and support their commitments and look to them to keep their oaths and say no to future illegal and/or immoral orders.

We are all in this together.

Chapter 1

A Profound and Abiding Debt of Gratitude

He always had to be worried about snipers.

They could take a soldier's life at any moment. And he had watched too many young men under his command take their last breaths after being shot by someone they would never see.

His men were often vulnerable targets as they labored both day and night to build and repair bridges, roads, and other infrastructure in support of combat troops. And then there were the planted explosive devices that could be anywhere and could detonate at any moment.

These were daily, relentless concerns for my father, Karl A. Johnson, as a 23-year-old Captain in the U.S. Army Corps of Engineers serving in both North Africa and Italy during World War II.

By the time "Victory Europe Day" (VE Day) arrived on May 8, 1945, he had written a total of thirty-two official condolences letters to the families of young soldiers. These same men had taken and upheld an oath to "support and defend the Constitution of the United States against all enemies, foreign and domestic …"

They risked their lives and lost them serving each other, their families, their friends, and their country. It did not matter what states they came from—they were all from the "United States of America." Most died never having been married or having children.

It's estimated that over 1.19 million American service members, men and women, have died since 1775, including both battle and non-combat deaths. Approximately 1.9 million Americans have received Purple Hearts in honor of injuries sustained in serving their country.

Presently, there are approximately 18 million veterans in the United States, all of whom, over the expanse of decades, took an oath to uphold the Constitution.

Four of the WWII deaths mentioned above were high school friends of my dad who died in separate, major battles in Europe. They gave their lives fighting against dictators, "strong men," who preached extreme nationalism, fear, and hatred, and who were enemies of democracy and fundamental civil rights.

They were not "suckers" and "losers" as Mr. Trump, during his first term, said to his Chief of Staff, Four-Star Marine General John Kelly, about the World War I soldiers who were buried at the Belleau Wood and Aisne-Marne American cemeteries in France.

If we were right now in the presence of those four brave young men from my dad's hometown of Chino, California, what would we say about the deep divisions in our country? How would we explain the events that led to the election of a president who is now systematically violating our Constitution, destroying our democratic republic, and attacking everyone and every organization that he considers "the enemy?"

Whatever we might say, they could reasonably ask, with the sincere, innocent, and slightly insecure look of young men in their twenties, "Thank you, but what are you going to do about it?" They might also ask whether their sacrifices might, ultimately, have been in vain.

On the day my father passed, November 19, 2019, he expressed great concern about the future of our country. Some 156 years earlier, also on November 19th, President Abraham Lincoln spoke eloquently about taking "increased devotion to the cause for which they gave their last full measure of devotion."

"Four score and seven years ago, our fathers brought forth, on this continent, a new nation, conceived in Liberty, and dedicated to the proposition that all men are created equal.

"Now we are engaged in a great civil war, testing whether that nation, or any nation so conceived and so dedicated, can long endure. We are met on a great battlefield of that war. We have come to dedicate a portion of that field, as a final resting place for those who here gave their lives that that nation might live. It is altogether fitting and proper that we should do this.

"But, in a larger sense, we cannot dedicate—we cannot consecrate—we cannot hallow—this ground. The brave men, living and dead, who struggled here, have consecrated it, far above our poor power to add or detract. The world will little note, nor long remember what we say here, but it can never forget what they did here. It is for us the living, rather, to be dedicated here to the unfinished work which they who fought here have thus far so nobly advanced. It is rather for us to be here dedicated to the great task remaining before us—that from these honored dead we take increased devotion to that cause for which they gave the last full measure of devotion—that we here highly resolve that these dead shall not have died in vain—that this nation, under God, shall have a new birth of freedom—and that

government of the people, by the people, for the people, shall not perish from the earth."
—Abraham Lincoln, The Gettysburg Address, November 19, 1863

Whether or not your ancestors, family, friends, or neighbors have ever served in the military, all Americans today have benefited from the freedom and benefits of a democratic republic and now face a historic and profound calling for "increased devotion" to the pursuit of common ground and the maintenance of our Union on the complex, highly divisive issues of our time.

A foundational, non-partisan starting point is to collectively and proudly affirm our support for the Constitution of the United States, with its revolutionary commitment to "equal protection" of the laws for all Americans and to a core government structure that balances powers between the legislative, executive, and judicial branches. Without "checks and balances" on governmental power, we are doomed to repeat thousands of years of human history by submitting to rule by dictators.

Concurrently, Americans also need to acknowledge that a democracy cannot function effectively or "long endure" when its citizens cannot be civil with one another and often fail to treat those with whom they disagree politely and respectfully. We need to soundly reject the continuing efforts to divide and conquer through lies, fear, anger, and the resulting lapse of necessary civil communications and the degradation of our democratic institutions.

Jennifer Frey, with the Fordham Institute, has written insightfully about what Founder Benjamin Franklin believed was a necessary prerequisite for effective democratic governance:

> "Benjamin Franklin, exiting the Constitutional Convention in 1787, was asked about the kind of government the delegates were creating. With characteristic wit and wisdom, he replied: 'A Republic, if you can keep it.'… Franklin, along with most of our founding fathers, believed that a democracy is only as good as its citizens, since democracy only flourishes with citizens who are capable of governing themselves. To quote Franklin again, 'only a virtuous people is capable of freedom' … Unfortunately, we have lost Franklin's understanding of the connection between virtue, self-government, and democracy."
> —Jennifer Frey, Civility and Democracy, The Thomas B. Fordham Inst. (2021), https://fordhaminstitute.org/national/commentary/civility-democracy-and-education.

As "should be" good citizens, many Americans in recent years have ignored the very real concerns of citizens in other states, including a seriously broken immigration system, the high cost of living, the national debt, inner city crime, and profound disagreement on a range of social and cultural issues.

Many good, moral Americans voted for Mr. Trump in 2024, often because their basic needs and top priorities were not being acknowledged and addressed. Only a small percentage of voters understood that Mr. Trump would, on day one, begin aggressively and comprehensively implementing Project 2025, a blueprint (consisting of 900+ pages) designed to establish a nationalist authoritarian regime.

Mr. Trump expressly and repeatedly disavowed any connection to Project 2025 during his campaign, and then promptly filled many key positions in his administration with people who were directly involved in creating that document and who are now busy with comprehensive implementation.

For those paying attention, the daily onslaught of unprecedented illegal and/or immoral acts has been and continues to be overwhelming. Project 2025 has an express goal of creating "chaos" and a resulting "paralysis" of the citizenry as power is progressively centralized, opposition is gradually eliminated, revenge is exacted against opponents, and everyone is on notice that they dare not disagree with its leader, Mr. Trump.

On the bright side, over 500 lawsuits have been filed to date by blue-state attorneys general, non-profit organizations, and individuals in response to the actions of the second Trump administration. Everyone is doing their best "to play defense," and we are seeing many successful results as a consequence of dedicated, highly skilled lawyers working tirelessly.

The Federal District Courts have been ruling, by some estimates, over 75% of the time in favor of the plaintiffs, but have often been overruled or their remedies stayed by appellate courts and the Supreme Court. And so, the illegal and immoral acts by Mr. Trump and his employees keep coming at the country and, in many cases, the world. They have been effectively "flooding the zone," to use a football term, in a calculated manner to overwhelm the system and the citizens.

It is high time to go on the offensive against Mr. Trump.

There is a reasonable legal path forward to have Mr. Trump declared in breach of what is basically his "Presidential Employment Contract" and to have that agreement rescinded—meaning, in lay terms, that Mr. Trump will be out of a job. This can be brought about through Constitution-based litigation using historical common law legal reasoning and related equitable remedies.

With our Constitution, we are blessed with one of the most important contracts in all human history. It is indeed a most unique, multi-dimensional contract that provides for and strives to protect individual rights for all Americans, sovereignty for states, conditional supremacy for the federal government, and at the same time, maintains a system of checks and balances that abhors centralized power.

It was always intended to be a "living and breathing" document that could adapt to advances in human knowledge, education, values, and science, and be "nimble" enough to logically and reasonably address the increasingly complex challenges that accompany these advances.

It's time to breathe new life into that contract to save us from the obvious, in-your-face, ongoing destruction of our democratic republic. Alongside this effort, we need nationwide public support and advocacy, sending a compelling message to all elected and appointed government employees in America that we will no longer look the other way, tolerate, or accept breaches of their oaths to uphold the Constitution.

And we owe these patriotic efforts to our families, friends, neighbors, to ourselves, to future generations, and to all those who are serving and have served our country in a wide variety of ways, especially those who gave their "last full measure of devotion" to protect our Union and our freedoms.

Chapter 2

Where Impeachment is not an Option

As we all know all too well, Mr. Trump has been impeached twice and, on both occasions, there were insufficient votes in the Senate to convict and remove him from office. Today, with the Republican majority in the Senate, there is no hope of a Senate conviction. Of course, Mr. Trump is taking illegal steps as we speak to maintain Republican control of the House so there can be no impeachment.

In tandem with this "dark history" and "gathering clouds," it is commonly believed that impeachment is the only way to remove Mr. Trump from office. This is incorrect.

Ever since people have entered into contracts, which is literally for thousands of years, circumstances have arisen where the original contract language does not expressly provide for a particular, timely, and reasonable solution for an unanticipated problem/dispute.

Laws have therefore developed over vast expanses of time to authorize the courts to read the content within the "four corners" of the document and to discern the best way to protect the expectations and rights of the parties to the agreement at the time of the disagreement. This is foundational contract law, and our Constitution is fundamentally a contract between the states and the federal government.

Accordingly, the presence of only one express remedy, i.e., impeachment, for ongoing, major breaches of the Presidential Oath is not, in itself, logically, morally, or legally a barrier to utilizing other enforcement mechanisms inherent in the contract that is our Constitution. Further, no historical precedent or authority suggests that the founders ever intended the country to be remediless when impeachment was not possible.

It is, in fact, fundamentally irrational to argue we have no choice but to suffer the consequences of a relentless series of unconstitutional orders, ongoing efforts to suppress and destroy our most fundamental rights, and daily pursuit of a publicly available plan, i.e., Project 2025, to dismantle our republic.

As stated compellingly by Professor Michael S. Paulsen:

> "The Constitution itself embraces an overriding principle of constitutional and national self-preservation that operates as a meta-rule of construction for the document's specific provisions … The Constitution is *not a suicide pact*; and, consequently, its provisions should not be construed to make it one, where an alternative construction is fairly possible. The Constitution should be construed to avoid constitutional implosion; it should not lightly be given a disabling, self-destructive interpretation.
> —Michael S. Paulsen, *The Constitution of Necessity*, 79 Notre Dame L. Rev. 1257 (2004); https://scholarship.law.nd.edu/ndlr/vol79/ iss4/3

In this regard, the subject of a prompt, meaningful response to a Presidential Oath violation was addressed before the Constitution was ratified. Writer James Sullivan commented on the subject in "Cassius VI. Mass. Gazette" on Dec. 21, 1787:

"[I]f [the President] should presume to deviate from [his oath] he would be immediately arrested in his career and summoned to answer for his conduct before a federal court."
—The Documentary History of the Ratification of the Constitution 500 (John P. Kaminski, et al. eds., 2009).

In good company with Mr. Sullivan's contract-oriented expectations, there is a long history of courts using common law principles to assist in constitutional interpretation and enforcement cases, fashioning remedies where they are not expressly provided for in a statute or the Constitution. (See "Constitutional Remedies: In One Era and Out the Other" by Professor Richard Fallon. Harvard Law Review, Vol. 136, Issue 5, pp. 1300-1366 March 2023).

Professor Fallon observes, primarily in the context of individual rights, that:

"[T]he Founding generation presupposed a background scheme of common law and equitable remedies through which the Constitution could be enforced and rights vindicated. The traditional law of constitutional remedies not only grew out of that background but also reflected its gradual adaptation to ensure effective enforcement of constitutional norms." (Id. 1323)

Regarding abuse of power by government officials, he notes:

> "If a single, central idea runs through discussions and debates about the rule of law, it is, accordingly, that the rule of law must somehow constrain officials as well as citizens and, in particular, must furnish a bulwark against official abuses of power. In light of that aim, a demand for enforcement of constitutional norms against government officials, typically if not invariably through judicial processes, lies within the core of any defensible conception." Id 1323.

The Conservative Point of View

This long history of common sense and adaptive interpretation and construction of the Constitution has been challenged and often rejected in recent decades by what are called originalist/textualist interpretations of the Constitution by conservative members of the Supreme Court. They routinely determine that if the Founders did not expressly write about an issue, then there is no remedy available through the Courts.

Former Supreme Court Associate Justice Stephen Breyer has thoughtfully commented on this trend in his recent book, *Reading the Constitution: Why I chose Pragmatism Not Textualism*. Therein, Justice Breyer observes:

> "The Constitution sets forth a structure and principles that aim to create and hold us together as a single nation for hundreds of years or more. I have approached the interpretive task with that fundamental objective in mind .... [B]y considering purposes, consequences, and values, I place less weight on the so-called plain meaning of a

statute or the Constitution than do many of my textualist colleagues. And I do so to arrive at an interpretation that is more faithful to the desire of the Constitution's Framers to establish a workable framework for long-lasting government." (Preface, xvii)

This approach is consistent with what Thomas Jefferson identified as a need for government to evolve with the times. As stated on the southeast wall of his Washington, D.C., memorial:

"I am not an advocate for frequent changes in laws and constitutions, but laws and institutions must go hand in hand with the progress of the human mind. As that becomes more developed more enlightened, as new discoveries are made, new truths discovered and manners and opinions change, with the change of circumstances institutions must advance also to keep pace with the times. We might as well require a man to wear still the coat that fitted him when a boy as civilized society to remain ever under the regime of their barbarous ancestors."

In lay terms, the so-called "originalists" and "textualists" modes of interpretation routinely reason their way into continuing to use the coat that, over 238 years ago, fit a child. Originalists focus on the ordinary meaning or intent of the words at the time they were chosen. Textualists concentrate on the ordinary meaning of the text with limited or no consideration of its intent or history. Both approaches routinely lead to the conclusion that there is no present remedy for a problem.

Regardless of the lawyerly, complex language of many recent conservative majority opinions, the usual result is to freeze the status quo, leaving us without solutions to our most pressing problems and typically prioritizing—without directly saying so—the rights of corporations and the rich and powerful over those of We the People.

The pragmatist approach, as explained by Justice Breyer, views the Constitution as a living and breathing document, designed to be flexible and adjustable to the times. This interpretive methodology includes a review of any relevant precedent (prior case law) and the "purposes, consequences, and values" involved with any proposed decision.

The President as an Employee

The president is an employee under a "quid pro quo" contract—something given in return for something else—activated by the promises made at the time of taking the Oath of Office and guided by the terms of the Constitution. U.S. Constitution, Article 2, Clauses 7 and 8; Carroll v. Trump, 49 F.4th 759; Black Lives Matter D.C. v. United States, 775 F.Supp.3d 241; 5 USCS Section 2105 (President as employee).

See also Corbin on Contracts, One Volume Edition, Chapter 1, Sections 1-13 (Defining components of a contract); And "The President as Officer Not Sovereign," Professor Bernadette Meyler, Harvard Law Review, Volume 133, Issue 4 (February 2020) (examining the scope of Presidential authority as constrained by the term "Office").

The terms of the Presidential Employment Contract are literally in the Constitution, which functionally provides for control over his employment by multiple employers—including We the People and the branches of the federal government—with different types, levels, and time-cycles of control over the employee.

We the People, through the states, elect the president, pay him with our taxes, and decide whether he gets a second term. We the People can exercise conditional, indirect control over the president through the Congress by advocating for and supporting impeachment in the House of Representatives and conviction through a trial in the Senate.

The Restatement (Third) of Agency Section 7.03 addresses multiple employers and allocation of termination rights. See Kelley v. Southern Pacific Co. 419 U.S. 318, 324 (1974) (addressing issue of "two masters simultaneously" in a National Labor Relations Board context.) See also Sandhu v. Board of Administration, etc. 108 Cal. App. 5th 1048, 1075-1077 (2025); Vernon v. State of California, 116 Cal. App. 4th 114, 125-129 (2004) (both addressing multiple employers and related control issues.)

Historic Use of Federal Common Law

Given the Presidential Employment Contract, it is logical and reasonable to apply common law contract principles and remedies to the unprecedented circumstances at hand. Further, federal courts around the country have historically and regularly used common law, established by prior case law, summarized and explained in an array of "Restatement Treatises."

In Gill v. Moco Thermal Industries, Inc. 981 F.2d 858 (1992), the Sixth Circuit applied federal common law of contracts to determine whether welfare benefits had vested. In County of Santa Clara v. Astra USA, Inc.

(2008) 540 F. 3d 1094(2008), the Ninth Circuit Court of Appeals relied upon the federal common law of contracts to support a right for federally funded medical clinics to enforce contracted discount pricing provisions against pharmaceutical companies.

In Wallach v. Eaton Corporation 837 F.3d 356 (2016), the Third Circuit applied the federal common law of contracts generally and the law of antitrust assignments specifically to address the validity of assignments of antitrust claims.

In Yee v. Jewell, 228 F.Supp.3d 48 (2017), the United States District Court, District of Columbia, in a suit against the U.S. Department of the Interior, confirmed that the "[F]ederal common law of contracts applies to contracts with the federal government ..."

Importantly, the U.S. Supreme Court has also historically relied upon Restatement law. In Community For Creative Non-Violence v. Reid 490 U.S.730, 752 n.31(1989), the Court relied upon the Restatement of Agency to help determine whether a sculpture was an "original work for hire" as defined by the Copyright Act of 1976 (17 U.S.C.S. Section 101).

In Burlington N. and Santa Fe Ry. Co. v. United States, 556 U.S. 599, 614-15(2009), the Supreme Court relied upon the Restatement (Second) of Torts Section 433A(1)(b) in determining a contamination liability apportionment issue under 42 U.S.C. Sections 9601-9675 ("CERCLA").

For an excellent overview of the historic use of common law in statutory interpretation, see Anita Krishnakumar, The Common Law as Statutory Backdrop, 136 Harv.L.Rev. 608, 610 (2022).

In contrast to this long history of common-law-assisted interpretation, the U.S. Supreme Court recently used a "textualist" approach to ignore several Restatements of Law to deny "standing" to the plaintiffs. The conservative majority found that no remedy was available to the injured parties. They essentially defended the status quo, denying relief and functionally freezing the Constitution in time.

In the case, Thole et al. v. U.S. Bank N.A. et al., 590 U.S. 538 (2020), Associate Justice Sonia Sotomayor authored an exhaustive and compelling dissent, joined by Associate Justices Bader, Breyer, and Kagan, in support of "standing" to sue management under Article III of the Constitution for participants in a defined-benefit retirement plan.

The dissent relied upon principles from the Restatement of the Law Third, Restitution and Unjust Enrichment; the Restatement of the Law Second, Trusts; the Restatement of the Law Third, Trusts; and the Restatement of the Law First, Contracts. (p.558-562)

Of particular relevance to the use of contracts precedents and standards, the dissent quoted from Section 328 of the Restatement (First):

"[B]reach of contract always create[d] a 'right of action,' even when no financial 'harm was caused.'" (p.561)

All things considered, based upon hundreds of years of legal precedent and solid legal reasoning, there is overwhelming evidence to support a Court finding that, among other things, Mr. Trump has materially breached his Presidential Employment Contract and that an appropriate remedy is rescission or withdrawal (nullification) of the contract.

A Partial List of Oath/Contract Breaches

Mr. Trump's oath/contract breaches, guided substantially by Project 2025 and designed to consolidate and permanently maintain power, have included:

1) The widespread suppression of 1st Amendment rights by defaming, slandering, threatening, investigating, extorting, indicting, and/or suing political opponents, universities, journalists, broadcast media, lawyers, law firms, transgender citizens, and, effectively, anyone who comes to his attention as having spoken out against his policies.

2) Denying due process and equal protection rights for hundreds of thousands of immigrants, including, at last count, approximately 170 citizens who were wrongfully arrested and incarcerated.

3) Shipping immigrants to countries they did not come from and where they are predictably in danger from political forces or are placed in brutal prison conditions.

4) Actively working to politicize the military by purging generals and admirals who are perceived as disloyal to Mr. Trump and removing access to military lawyers who have historically advised the Armed Forces on possible illegal orders.

5) Turning Immigration and Customs Enforcement (ICE) into a massively funded and armed paramilitary organization controlled exclusively by Mr. Trump and using armed, masked agents every day to scare and often brutally arrest people of color.

6) Pursuing through ICE and other government agencies unprecedented surveillance capabilities to be used against private citizens in suppression of their 1st Amendment rights.

7) Illegally nationalizing state National Guard troops and deploying them into "Democratic cities" under

pretenses, facilitated by half-truths and lies by Department of Justice (DOJ) lawyers alleging non-existent violence and circumstances beyond the control of law enforcement.

8) Actively moving to "rig" and control the outcome of the mid-term elections through unprecedented, coordinated, anti-democratic gerrymandering; overt voter suppression tactics, including, it appears, plans to have troops deployed in Democratic cities as part of an effort to keep people away from the polls.

9) Attacking foreign countries (Iran) without the consent of Congress and targeting alleged drug cartel boats and killing people with no proof and no due process.

10) Unilaterally threatening invasions of foreign countries (Venezuela and Greenland) without the consent of Congress or the support of the people.

11) Frequently ignoring court orders on a wide variety of matters.

12) Threatening judges who ruled against his executive orders with impeachment, when that remedy is only available for "high crimes and misdemeanors," and knowing his threats lead to physical threats by his supporters against judges, their staff, and, in some cases, their families.

Over 120 Executive Orders

Mr. Trump has repeatedly issued unconstitutional or otherwise illegal executive orders, averaging ten per month. The White House and, all too often, the media refer to Mr. Trump's orders as actions "testing the limits of his executive authority." This usually means that Mr. Trump has issued an executive order inviting the Supreme Court to functionally and illegally amend the Constitution or long-standing federal statutes that have explicit language and are supported by thoughtful, non-prejudiced precedent.

Birthright Citizenship, for example, is a Constitutional right clearly stated and backed by well-reasoned, extensive case law dating back to the nineteenth century. (See e.g. *United States v. Wong Kim Ark* 169 U.S. 649, 649 (1898).

Mr. Trump, on the first day back in office, issued an executive order purporting to end birthright citizenship because he is openly prejudiced against non-white immigrants. They have been targets of Mr. Trump for years and a focus of his continuing campaign of fear and division, designed in part to justify the often brutal and inhumane tactics of Immigration and Customs Enforcement (ICE).

The only legal way to end birthright citizenship is to amend, through a state ratification process, the plain language of the Constitution. Existing case law explaining the plain language can only be overruled appropriately when there are evident flaws in the reasoning or the decision was motivated by prejudicial or other improper motives.

None of these circumstances are present here, and yet Mr. Trump, from day one, has been directing the massive powers of the federal government against immigrants in various settings, even when they are documented or are citizens, and including several times where they have been personally targeted for exercising 1st Amendment rights opposing administration policies.

This premeditated and ongoing illegal conduct against people of color essentially assumes there is no birthright citizenship nor equal protection. It is therefore directly inconsistent with the Presidential Oath to "faithfully execute" the Office of the President and his concurrent obligation to ensure that the laws are faithfully executed by everyone working for the administration.

Another example of a requested illegal Constitutional amendment issued through a unilateral executive order involves Mr. Trump's widespread and often arbitrary imposition of tariffs. Only Congress has the power to tax, and tariffs have always been considered a tax since the beginning.

Tellingly, even though Trump controls majorities in both houses, he did not bother to ask Congress to vote for tariffs. He just levied them and has been collecting tens of billions of dollars with massive impacts around the world. He is, as in the case of birthright citizenship, acting in bad faith and beyond the scope of his articulated powers in the Constitution.

Judicial Perspectives

Stepping back and looking at the overwhelming numbers of Mr. Trump's illegal and bad faith actions and the millions of people his conduct has negatively impacted, it is reasonable to assume there are large numbers of federal district court judges, and federal circuit court justices, including many Trump appointees, who will be courageous enough to rule in favor of Mr. Trump losing his job.

Federal District Court Judge Mark R. Wolf, a Reagan appointee who had been on the bench since 1985, recently stepped down from his lifetime appointment with the following explanation:

> "My reason is simple: I no longer can bear to be restrained by what judges can say publicly or do outside the courtroom. President Donald Trump is using the law for partisan purposes, targeting his adversaries while sparing his friends and donors from investigation, prosecution, and

possible punishment. This is contrary to everything I have stood for in my more than fifty years in the Department of Justice and on the bench. The White House's assault on the rule of law is so deeply disturbing to me that I feel compelled to speak out. Silence, for me, is now intolerable." Mark R. Wolf, Why I Am Resigning, *The Atlantic*, (Nov. 9, 2025), https://www.theatlantic.com/ideas/2025/11/federal-judge-resignation-trump/684845/.

We can readily assume that Judge Wolf reflects the outlook of the vast majority of judges on the federal bench, which presently totals 670, of whom 187 (or 28%) are Trump appointees.

Importantly, initiating the proposed breach-of-contract lawsuits and having them pending could create a form of "second thought guardrails" around Mr. Trump and members of his administration, as, practically speaking, every further act in violation of his oath will add to the evidence against him.

At this moment, Mr. Trump considers himself untouchable.

The proposed breach-of-contract litigation will loudly say he is not.

The Cumulative Impacts of Mr. Trump's Actions and Words

A crucial distinction here, compared to the now over 500 hundred defensive (meaning in response to specific illegal actions) lawsuits now pending against Mr. Trump and/or his administration, is that the recommended, breach of oath contract cases against Mr. Trump can be based upon the cumulative impacts of all or many of his breaches and, critically, they seek what might be called a "global remedy" where Mr. Trump's employment contract is just ended.

In traditional contract law terms, a single act of illegal misconduct might not be considered actionable. However, the circumstances, details, and the *cumulative* impact of all the misconduct on the aggrieved party can support a finding of material breach supporting an appropriate remedy. Restatement (Second) of Contracts, Section 241; Hometown Fin., Inc. v. United States, 60 Fed.Ct. 513 (2005).

Mr. Trump's recent social media postings, including the statement that Democrats are in a party of "hate, evil and Satan" and his in-person address to the entire military leadership of the United States imploring them to prepare to battle the "enemy within"—i.e., his opponents—are compelling, beyond-frightening, and indisputable examples of his commitment to dividing and conquering the United States.

These statements are additional robust evidence to place in front of the courts, which only have to decide in a civil contract matter whether it is "more probable than not" that Mr. Trump has materially breached his oath and therefore his Presidential Employment Contract. Proof beyond a reasonable doubt, as required in a criminal case, is not required under the proposed civil litigation strategy.

Other vital evidence to be used in the breach-of-contract cases will be the Project 2025 documents—disavowed by Mr. Trump during his campaign—which express an extreme nationalist blueprint for building an authoritarian presidency.

In using the term "nationalist," I have in mind a concise and thoughtful explanation by Episcopal Priest Joseph Yoo, who has distinguished "patriotism" from "nationalism." "Patriotism says, 'I love my family enough to admit when we've messed up, and I will help us grow. Nationalism says, "My family is perfect, everyone else is trash, and if you disagree, you are out." John Yoo, Our Anticompetitive Patriotism, 39 U.C. Davis L. Rev. 1243 (2006).

In this vein, American humorist Mark Twain famously commented, "Patriotism is supporting your country all the time and your government when it deserves it." Mark Twain, The Czar's Soliloquy, N. Am. Rev., Mar. 1905, at 345

Since the first day of the second Trump term, the project goals have been actively pursued and are reportedly about 47% of the way toward completion. (See "Project 2025.Observer"; "ProgressiveReform.org"; "naacpldf.org" (tracking project—2025). This aggressive, comprehensive, and detailed course of conduct, steadily dismantling our democratic republic, leaves no doubt whatsoever about Mr. Trump's intentions both before and after he took the Oath of Office

Reading the Supreme Court

There is overwhelming evidence that Mr. Trump and his administration have engaged in an ongoing lawless and often cruel pursuit of his own authoritarian power, wealth, and vengeance. Accordingly, there is a reasonable possibility that a five-to-four majority of the Supreme Court Justices would vote to effectuate the loss of Mr. Trump's employment or to establish some form of meaningful guardrails on Mr. Trump's future behavior and the conduct of future presidents—a critical long-term consideration.

In this regard, review of Supreme Court voting records shows that Chief Justice Roberts and Associate Justice Barrett, and perhaps Kavanaugh, could join the three progressive Justices in a favorable vote. These Justices have demonstrated a degree of moderation in some of their rulings, particularly in their approach to the balance-of-powers structure of the Constitution. Further, there is no historical evidence to conclude they have been lifelong, closeted monarchists or neo-authoritarian proponents.

No doubt they all favor a limited federal government, strong states' rights, and a powerful executive, but that does not mean they want to see our entire democratic republic destroyed. They know Mr. Trump is often out of control in his public statements and actions, and they know that their June 2024 decision on Presidential Immunity for criminal activity has played a significant role in Mr. Trump's ongoing lawlessness.

At the same time, as human beings, most of them must worry, to one degree or another, about prospective public attacks from Mr. Trump that will and have led to death threats against them and some family members. Similarly, as members of the highest court in the land, they all must be concerned about Mr. Trump impulsively deciding to ignore all future court orders.

In this practical context, we might think of these Justices as managing the temperature of a teapot that is warming, incrementally giving Trump partial or complete victories to avoid dangerous overheating or catastrophic overreaction.

For an excellent article about the complexities of the challenges and pressures presented to the Supreme Court Justices by Mr. Trump's actions, and the possibility of future, favorable rulings on such key balance-of-power issues as tariffs and Federal Reserve Commissioner independence, see "The Supreme Court's Trump Enablers...." by attorney Simon Lazarus. "Smart News.com" 9/24/25.

How they would rule on a breach of the Presidential Employment Contract lawsuit, however, will also depend upon what else Trump does in the coming months, the then current perceptions or facts about his physical and mental health, and the extent to which other people, governments, businesses and institutions, including the military, demonstrate their loyalty to the Constitution and not Mr. Trump.

Assessing Each Other's Commitment to the Constitution

It is important for everyone to be encouraged by the National Guard units from various states complying with court orders regarding deployments in Democratic Cities. It is totally wrong of course that they are there in the first place, but they are respecting the rule of law, versus the rule of Mr. Trump.

This is additionally important because many of the guard units are from Red States and no doubt have many soldiers who are, generally speaking, Donald Trump supporters. So thank you to the leadership of those guard units for following the Courts. They are respecting the Constitution and setting a most important example for the entire country, including all the other state national guards, to see and to follow in the future.

Overall, every institution and every individual in a position of power, civil or military, needs to believe that they have "each other's back" in fully supporting our

Constitution, which includes following the orders of the courts, especially when those orders go against Mr. Trump.

In this context, individual acts of integrity and courage that oppose illegal and/or unethical orders should always have the attention of the independent media and our mutual respect. The recently demonstrated courage of the Trump-appointed U.S. Attorney Erik K. Siebert in Virginia, who refused to indict New York Attorney General Leticia James for lack of evidence, is one inspiring example. Siebert also formally recommended against indicting former FBI Director James Comey. He was then basically forced to resign after Trump threatened to fire him.

The unexpected success of late-night host Jimmy Kimmel, along with multitudes of vocal Americans, in convincing ABC and Disney that his show should be reinstated delighted and inspired millions. The more people stand up for the principles of the Constitution, the more others will be inspired to say "no" to any number of improper, immoral, or illegal directives.

Of course, no one knows precisely where the country will be in six months or a year. Still, common sense and prudence strongly counsel moving now to initiate the litigation necessary to place the breach and fraud issues before the courts so that the Supreme Court Justices, sooner than later, have an opportunity to do the right thing.

In this unique, dynamic, and even dangerous environment, it is hard to predict how long a contract case, or any of its components, might take to reach the Supreme Court. Under one procedural scenario, key issues could be there within ninety days, so if one were filed in January of 2026, the Court could see it in the late Spring. One of many alternative scenarios would be not reaching the Court for a year or more.

Regardless of the eventual interim or final outcomes before the Supreme Court, the proposed lawsuit(s) will create a unique opportunity to educate the American people about the Constitution, including the Presidential Oath—the only one in the Constitution—and the critical importance of good faith adherence to all oaths taken by Americans around the country.

Chapter 3

Breach of the Presidential Oath of Office and the Faithful Execution Clause

Article II, Section 1, Clause 8 of the Constitution states:

> "Before he enters on the Execution of his Office, he shall take the following Oath or Affirmation:
> "I do solemnly swear (or affirm) that I will *faithfully execute* the Office of the President of the United States, and will to the best of my ability, preserve, protect and defend the Constitution of the United States."

In addition, Article II, Section 3 provides in part that the president:

> "[S]hall take care that the Laws be *faithfully executed* …"

This Section 3 directive is commonly referred to as the "Take Care" clause. Simply stated, this section imposes a duty on the president to ensure that the people working for him are faithfully executing the laws in their respective areas of responsibility.

The history and original meaning of these "Faithful Execution Clauses" were comprehensively examined by Professors Leib, Handelsman-Shugerman, and Kent in a Harvard Law Review article, Volume 132, Issue 8, June 2019, entitled "Faithful Execution and Article II."

Going back to the Magna Carta ("the Great Charter") in 1215 England, which limited the power of the King, and tracing subsequent centuries of legal precedent, historical practices and writings through the time of the Constitutional Convention in 1787—a process that textualists and originalists should respect—they convincingly concluded there were "three duties of fidelity" under the concept of Faithful Execution:

> "(1)) a duty not to act ultra vires, beyond the scope of one's office; (2) a duty not to misuse an office's funds or take unauthorized profits; and (3) diligent, careful, good faith, honest, and impartial execution of law or office." (page 2111)

> They also commented that: "These three duties of fidelity look a lot like fiduciary duties in the modern private law." (Id.)

This latter insight is material to the Presidential Employment Contract because even without express terms like "Faithful Execution," modern common law provides that employees implicitly have duties of good faith, fidelity, and loyalty to their employers, and depending upon the specific circumstances, a fiduciary duty, which imposes even higher standards of performance. Restatement (Second) Contracts, Chapter 7, Section 161, comment (f.); Chapter 2, Section 9, comment (b).

Based upon the well-known facts of Mr. Trump's conduct before, during, and after the inauguration ceremony on January 20, 2025, we see a President-elect who, in a premeditated manner, had detailed plans, in cooperation with an unknown number of people and organizations, to ignore the "Faithful Execution Clauses." And since the day that power was turned over to him, the nation and world have witnessed an overwhelming onslaught of breaches of the "three duties of fidelity" with the clearly expressed goal of destroying our freedoms and our democratic republic.

What then are the specific legal theories and remedies appropriate for addressing these ongoing violations of the Constitution?

Fraud in the Inducement, Restatement (Second) of Contracts

Chapter 7. "Misrepresentation, Duress, and Undue Influence" includes multiple sections addressing the actionable circumstances related to misrepresentation and Mr. Trump's misconduct matches up well with several of these section topics:

> Section 160. When Action is Equivalent to An Assertion (Concealment)
> Section 161. When Non-Disclosure is Equivalent to An Assertion
> Section 162. When A Misrepresentation Is Fraudulent Or Material
> Section 164. When a Misrepresentation Makes A Contract Voidable
> Section 167. When A Misrepresentation Is An Inducing Cause

> Section 167 reads as follows:
> "A misrepresentation induces a party's manifestation of assent if it substantially contributes to his decision to manifest his assent."

Fundamentally, we know that Donald Trump lied when he took the oath to preserve, protect, and defend the Constitution. From an evidentiary standpoint, and somewhat bizarrely, it is very significant that Mr. Trump chose not to place his hand on a Bible, even though his wife was holding two Bibles, one of which was reportedly used by Abraham Lincoln when he was sworn in as President in 1861.

How ironic.

The evidence against Mr. Trump for *fraud in the inducement* under Section 167 is overwhelming. And under a civil case burden of proof, the plaintiff only needs to show, with evidence, that it is more probable than not (at least 51% to 49%) that Mr. Trump, in taking the Oath of Office, made material misrepresentations to induce a transfer of power.

He, in fact, made false statements to everyone watching, including the Chief Justice of the Supreme Court, the outgoing President and Vice President, retiring Cabinet members, Congressional leadership, State Representatives, and to all Americans—all to induce the transfer of power.

With the compelling evidence of fraud in this case, Section 164 of The Restatement (Second) of Contracts provides that the contract is "voidable," or, in lay terms, no longer exists:

> "(1) If a party's manifestation of assent is induced by either a fraudulent or material misrepresentation by the other party upon which the recipient is justified in relying, the contract is voidable by the recipient."

Regarding justified reliance, it is reasonable to ask if those witnessing the oath and acquiescing to the transfer of power reasonably relied upon Mr. Trump's oath. "Comment; a. Scope" for Section 167 suggests that even if there was some skepticism on the part of those present, it is enough that the taking of the oath "substantially contributed" to the decision by everyone relinquishing power to consent to the contract.

Factually, on January 20, 2025, the people acquiescing to and participating in the "peaceful transfer of power" were first and foremost seeking to demonstrate respect for the election results. They were also hoping for some degree of compliance with the Oath of Office and that our system of checks and balances would be effective in restraining Mr. Trump's conduct.

No one reasonably anticipated that the ongoing, comprehensive, detailed, anti-democratic, immoral, often cruel, and retaliatory "blitzkrieg" would be carried out by Mr. Trump using every level of government. No one anticipated that Mr. Trump would convince Congress to fund billions of dollars to turn ICE into a massive, paramilitary force with required loyalty to Mr. Trump.

Mr. Trump has surprised even his most vocal critics. In the event his employment contract is declared "void" at the inception, there would be a reasonable argument that all of Mr. Trump's executive orders are invalid and inoperative, having been issued by an unauthorized individual.

The validity of an executive order is dependent upon the signing authority having the underlying legal authority. The legal power must come from a statute or the Constitution. Youngstown Sheet and Tube Co. v. Sawyer, 343 U.S. 579, 585 (1952); AFGE, AFL-CIO v. Trump, 139 F.4th 1020, 1034 (2025); Panama Refining Co. v. Ryan,

293 U.S. 388, 433 (1935); Cole v.Young, 351 U.S. 536, 559 (1956). In the case of Mr. Trump, the argument would be that he had no legal power from the Constitution nor a statute as his employment contract was never in effect nor operable.

Material Breaches of Contract, Restatement (Second) of Contracts

Given the now 500-plus lawsuits brought to date against Donald Trump and/or the federal government and the success rate, the evidence is overwhelming that Mr. Trump is aggressively pursuing his goal of dismantling our system of checks and balances and consolidating his own power. He continues to breach his Presidential Employment Contract with no end in sight.

There are a variety of contract remedies available for material breaches, as the courts have considerable leeway in fashioning equitable remedies. They can, as alluded to earlier, order contract rescission, which returns the parties to their pre-contract positions. Restatement (Second) of Contracts, Chapter 16. Remedies, Sections 344-385.

Under "Comment" for Section 358, it provides: (a) Flexibility of order. The objective of the court in granting equitable relief is to do complete justice to the extent that this is feasible. Under the rule stated in Subsection (1), the court has the power to mold its order to this end. The form and terms of the order are to a considerable extent within the discretion of the court.

Under Section 359, Effect of Adequacy of Damages, Comment c., the rescission remedy is expressly identified: "The availability of other forms of equitable relief, such as a decree for specific restitution, for reformation, and for <u>rescission</u> (underscore added), or cancellation, may also be considered in choosing the remedy best suited to the circumstances of the case."

Restatement (Third) of Restitution and Unjust Enrichment, Chapter 4. Restitution and Contract, Section 37 Rescission and Material Breach, subsection 1 provides in relevant part that "[A] plaintiff who is entitled to a remedy for the defendant's material breach *or* (italics added) repudiation may choose rescission as an alternative to enforcement …"

Breach of the Duty of Good Faith and Fair Dealing, Restatement (Second) of Contracts

Section 205, Chapter 9 – THE SCOPE OF CONTRACTUAL OBLIGATIONS, Duty of Good Faith and Fair Dealing, provides: "Every contract imposes upon each party a duty of good faith and fair dealing in its performance and its enforcement, and Comment (e) ... Good faith in enforcement. The obligation of good faith and fair dealing extends to the assertion, settlement and litigation of contract claims and defenses … The obligation is violated by dishonest conduct such as conjuring up a pretended dispute, asserting an interpretation contrary to one's understanding, or *falsification of facts."* (emphasis added)

In this regard, it is important that Mr. Trump has fictionalized large-scale civil violence, and his lawyers have lied or exaggerated about alleged violence on the streets in Portland, Chicago, Los Angeles, Memphis, and Washington, D.C. They have been called out directly by district court judges for misrepresentations to the courts about the need for military deployment for civil law enforcement.

In considering whether the Duty of Good Faith and Fair Dealing has been breached, in any situation, and what the appropriate remedies might be, Section 207 of the Restatement (Second) of Contracts provides: "In choosing among the reasonable meanings of a promise or agreement or a term thereof, a meaning that serves the public interest is generally preferred."

Overall, a contract rescission remedy is clearly appropriate in response to the comprehensive, intentional, and continuing bad faith breaches of the Presidential Oath of Office.

There is, however, another legal approach to obtaining rescission based upon expected future breaches of contract. It's called "repudiation."

Mr. Trump's ongoing, public maneuvers, including conspiratorial gerrymandering, voter suppression related to mail-in ballots, citizenship identification, and present and future voter intimidation through illegal use of the military, all appear to be designed to ensure he does not lose control of Congress in the November 2026 midterms. These actions and many others that are being objected to in the courts and elsewhere are reasonably viewed, collectively, as ongoing "repudiation" of the terms of this Presidential Employment Contract and are reasonably considered an independent ground for court-ordered rescission.

To help educate the public and lay the best possible evidentiary groundwork for this legal approach, anyone who is prepared to litigate against Mr. Trump should formally ask Mr. Trump, both publicly and in writing, to provide express assurances that he will not continue with any number of material breaches. This approach can be considered a form of equitable "exhaustion of remedies," in which plaintiffs inform the future defendant specifically of their issues, and the recipient, in turn, has an opportunity to correct the problem.

Mr. Trump will predictably reject or repudiate the request by words or deeds, and accordingly, the principles below from Chapter 10 of the Restatement (Second) will clearly apply both legally and equitably.

Repudiation And Assurance of Performance, Restatement (Second) of Contracts

Chapter 10, Performance and Non-Performance, Restatement (Second) of Contracts, Section 250. When A Statement Or Act Is A Repudiation, Comment b. provides: "Nature of statement. In order to constitute a repudiation, a party's language must be sufficiently positive to be reasonably interpreted to mean that the party will not or cannot perform. Mere expression of doubt as to his willingness or ability to perform is not enough to constitute a repudiation, although such an expression may give an obligee reasonable grounds to believe that the obligor will commit a serious breach and may ultimately result in a repudiation under the rule stated in section 251."

Section 251 (2) provides: "The obligee may treat as a repudiation the obligor's failure to provide within a reasonable time such assurance of due performance as is adequate in the circumstances of the particular case."

As stated in *Corbin on Contracts, One Volume Edition,* Section 984:

> "Repudiation is a manifestation of intention not to perform a contractual duty ... It has become a proverb that actions speak louder than words. Therefore, if a promisor so conducts himself as to

make the substantial performance of his promise impossible, this is a repudiation of his promise and has the same legal effect as would a repudiation in words." (p.969)

Given the ongoing "blitzkrieg" of Constitutional violations by Mr. Trump, there can be any number of requests for "assurance of due performance." Subsequent lawsuits could, for example focus on repudiation of demand for respecting 5th Amendment Due Process for both citizens and non-citizens, respecting states' rights to conduct their own elections, respecting birthright citizenship, respecting existing clear limits on when the U.S. military can be used on domestic soil, respecting the exclusive right of Congress to declare War, and/or respecting the 1st Amendment rights of his political opponents.

A most deserving effort would be to announce and send requests for assurances that the President will promptly order ICE agents to stop wearing masks at all times, as the face coverings are clearly intended to scare and intimidate people and to make accountability for misconduct very difficult or impossible.

Mr. Trump's Mental Health

Another important use of the principle of assurance of due performance would be a formal written request, backed up by detailed letters from qualified medical professionals and even letters from Trump relatives, for Mr. Trump to prove through independent medical experts that he is not suffering from debilitating dementia or an equivalent mental disability—periodic or continuous—due to ongoing physical processes.

He, of course, will reject the request and continue to insist that he is in perfect health. This response could reasonably be characterized as a repudiation of his duty, pursuant to his Oath of Office to conduct himself honestly and in good faith. Further, as expressed in the 25th Amendment, he must be able to "discharge the powers and duties of his office."

Once in court, admissible evidence would include video recordings, transcripts, and social media posts reflecting Mr. Trump's progressive decline.

In cases of alleged mental incapacity in other civil settings, a district court judge routinely has the power to order an independent medical exam with the medical professional(s) reporting back directly to the court. In this "presidential" context, there is a compelling state interest in knowing whether, for example, the person with his "finger on the nuclear trigger" has impaired judgment due to a physical illness or a medication regimen, or if he is mentally disabled to some material degree.

These questions are also important with respect to prospective 3:00 a.m. decisions to attack foreign countries or civilian fishing boats without evidence to confirm the action is justified and legal. Similarly, Mr. Trump has just ordered the U.S. to start testing nuclear weapons with a frequency commensurate with the testing practices of China, Russia, and North Korea. With his track record of doubling down after negative responses from recipients of his aggression, the issue of mental stability is even more critical

We often see his ego, rhetoric, and judgment appear out of control. With the ongoing "retirements" of experienced generals, we have no assurance that anyone will be present to restrain him with logic, historical perspective or reference to applicable laws governing the use of the military.

Then there is the issue of directions to ICE without active-duty military advice or participation. And for those who will strenuously object to a court-ordered mental exam as not being expressly authorized by the Constitution, I would remind them that the document is not to be read as a suicide pact.

The legal briefing in an incapacity repudiation case would include a full quotation of Section 4 of the 25th Amendment, which provides a remedy to formally declare that the "President is unable to discharge the powers and duties of his office." U.S. Const. amend. XXV, § 4. As with the remedy of impeachment under Article II, it is not presently available because Mr. Trump completely controls those expressly authorized to exercise the option. Once again, we need to pursue a reasonable legal avenue to effectuate a required remedy to protect We the People and our democratic republic.

Chapter 4

Conspiratorial Bad Actors, Pardons, and Emoluments

The offensive legal strategy suggested here includes widespread consideration of sending notices of possible claims against key people who are helping Mr. Trump violate his Oath of Office. Formal notice and the selective pursuit of such claims could help establish some degree of guardrails for the future conduct of his "employees."

Many of them have taken an oath, routinely violate it, and their conduct is often clearly outside their official duties, so any assertions of immunity from civil and or criminal liability should not be successful. For example, Democrats on the House Judiciary Committee recently wrote to officials at the Department of Justice regarding Mr. Trump's meritless claims for reimbursement of $230 million in legal fees expended in defending suits brought by the previous DOJ. They cautioned that a formal DOJ opinion approving the claims would constitute a violation of their oaths to uphold the Constitution and bring "personal consequences." They specifically stated:

> "You could face civil liability, ethics investigations, professional discipline, and potential criminal liability for conspiracy to defraud the United States."
> (Letter from Ranking Member Jamie Raskin and Judiciary Committee Democrats to Attorney General Pam Bondi, Deputy Attorney General Todd Blanche, and Associate Attorney General

Stanley Woodward (Oct. 28, 2025), https://democrats-judiciary.house.gov/media-center/press-releases/judiciary-democrats-expand-probe-demand-doj-officials-reject-president-s-corrupt-demand-for-230-million-payout.)

Similar notices from other aggrieved parties, to, for example, leaders and actors within ICE, directing the daily brutal tactics of ICE, would also be useful.

Trump's appointees and other employees in all government departments appear to believe they are untouchable because Trump is in power, plans to be there for a long time, substantially controls the Supreme Court, and he or a successor would pardon them if they became the target of criminal or civil litigation.

One way to address this untouchable perception is to bring civil lawsuits directly against bad-acting government employees. Depending on the specific facts, lawsuits could be brought against them as co-conspirators in the commission of civil wrongs or as parties to a civil conspiracy.

There are four elements to a civil conspiracy claim: 1) one person entered into an agreement with another person or persons; 2) to commit a tort—usually some personal injury—or another legal wrong, 3) a specific act was taken pursuant to the agreement; and 4) the conspiracy target incurred some harm, economic or otherwise, as a result of the unlawful act or tort.

Looking, for example, at the ongoing unlawful and egregious conduct of ICE around the country, those agents are working together, i.e., conspiring, with their bosses and through them, Mr. Trump, to seize and deport immigrants around the country, not caring about probable cause or due process protections for anyone they target, even if they happen to be legal American citizens.

A standard seizure effort by ICE agents typically involves an imposing armed man, without ID and wearing a mask, confronting an individual and making them feel threatened (an assault); that agent then grabs the person (a battery); and the person is then handcuffed and wrongly taken away to some form of detention center (false imprisonment), These are three distinct, actionable legal wrongs each of which can be a basis for a civil conspiracy claim against the perpetrators.

Several legal privileges traditionally protect federal law enforcement employees from liability, and careful consideration should be given to the applicability of existing statutory, regulatory, and case law in light of the unprecedented circumstances of the moment. However, just as there needs to be remedies for Trump's illegal conduct, there are compelling needs for remedies against his "Generals," his "foot soldiers," and everyone in between. And as the present circumstances are so manifestly unprecedented, prior case law is subject to being deemed by the courts distinguishable and not controlling.

Standards for Presidential Pardons

Another realm of presidential power that appears to involve numerous violations of the "three duties of fidelity" is the power of pardon. Mr. Trump has a long history of dangling and giving pardons in exchange for a wide range of considerations—i.e., acts or forbearances of conduct of value to him. The case law on the proper scope of pardons is quite limited, and unfortunately, there is a general perception that the president can pardon whoever he wants for whatever reason.

This notion is fundamentally misplaced because, as we have seen, our Constitution does not create a king with unlimited powers. The president is to be bound by his oath, which commits him to the three duties of fidelity. Offering pardons to criminals for past, present, or future political or economic considerations is not authorized directly or indirectly by any reasonable application of those standards.

In this regard, Professors Kent, Leib, and Shugerman, in their Harvard Law Review Article "Faithful Execution and Article II," have suggested that:

> "[T]he Take Care Clause and Presidential Oath clause also speak to contemporary controversies about President Trump's use of the pardon power and his control over removal of officers in the Department of Justice." Harvard Law Review, Volume 132, Issue 8, June 2019, p. 2116 (Faithful Execution and Article II).

The act of offering pardons in advance of bargained-for misconduct should be considered a particularly egregious violation of the Presidential Oath. It could constitute a civil conspiracy, depending upon the foreseeable consequences of the specific bargained-for misconduct.

Offering, in theory, a pardon to Ghislaine Maxwell, in return for her silence on the content of the Epstein files and her memories as an eyewitness, would be reasonably adjudicated as illegal when gauged by the three duties of fidelity. Victims of the Epstein misconduct would likely have standing to bring suits in federal court seeking to have any such pardon declared invalid.

The victims of the January 6th defendants pardoned by Trump would be logical plaintiffs to litigate against Mr.

Trump and those he has pardoned, particularly if there were direct or indirect evidence of quid pro quo, such as Mr. Trump expecting the recipients to, so to speak, "Stand back and stand by."

Any litigation in this Jan. 6th insurrection pardon arena should raise the issue of whether there was any form of good-faith review of the likelihood of future crimes by a pardon candidate. It seems highly unlikely, especially when one considers that at least ten of those pardoned for their January 6th criminal acts have been "rearrested, charged or sentenced for other crimes." (*Citizens for Responsibility & Ethics in Wash., CREW Statement on January 6th Pardons* (Jan. 20, 2025), https://www.citizensforethics.org/news/press-releases/crew-statement-on-january-6th-pardons/)

As recently as November 2, 2025, in a "60 Minutes" interview, Mr. Trump stated that he knew nothing about the billionaire he had recently pardoned. Yet that billionaire had previously been convicted of money laundering through a cryptocurrency exchange he founded, which now hosts the Trump family's crypto business.

Common sense, fairness, and justice require express, enforceable criteria for the granting of pardons, with particular attention to apparent conflicts of interest both before and after a pardon. Using the three duties of fidelity is a most logical and reasonable approach to satisfying this need.

Emoluments and Self-Enrichment

In addition to oath-violation-based challenges regarding civil conspiracies and pardons, it could be asserted that ongoing self-enrichment/emolument abuses by Mr. Trump constitute independent grounds for finding material breach of his employment contract.

Article 1, Section 9, "The Foreign Emoluments Clause," gifts from foreign powers without congressional approval; and Article II, Section 1, Clause 7, "The Domestic Emoluments Clause," prohibit compensation beyond the presidential salary from the U.S. government and the states.

Nearly every week, it seems there is news of Mr. Trump and his family members making deals with foreign or domestic businesses in which they have direct, indirect, or prospective financial interests. Foreign money regularly flows to Trump's businesses and properties overseas. In this context, there are also examples of government contracts being awarded to companies connected, directly or indirectly to Trump family interests.

His recent claim for compensation for $230 million in alleged attorney fees incurred in the defense of his criminal cases stemming from the Jan. 6th insurrection and the theft of secret government documents is a shocking example of him using his presidential power to try to illegally extract funds from the federal government and, therefore, the taxpayers.

His use of government lawyers to defend over 500 lawsuits that have been filed against his illegal actions in his second term raises serious questions about the taxpayers' rights to recover the value of those fees in cases where he has knowingly been taking unconstitutional or otherwise illegal actions in pursuit of authoritarian powers or, as is often the case, revenge against perceived enemies.

As is commonly observed, everything is a transaction for Mr. Trump. By all appearances and actions, he is continuously focusing on using his government position to enrich and empower himself and members of his family. He is also remarkably and tragically committed to seeking revenge against political opponents and anyone he feels has wronged him.

Previous emoluments litigation against Mr. Trump during his first term was either dismissed on grounds that there were not sufficient details in the Constitution to enforce the mandates (sound familiar?) or that the relief sought was moot because Trump was soon leaving office. See *In re Trump*, 926 F.3d 360 (2019).

Pursuing Mr. Trump now on a breach of contract claim for his emoluments abuses steps around these previous precedents, which also, like nearly every other case decided since Mr. Trump's first term, are readily distinguishable in terms of the now unprecedented factual circumstances.

Chapter 5

Presidential Immunity, Standing to Sue, and Public Advocacy

In Trump v. United States, 603 U.S. 593 (2024), the Supreme Court ruled that:

> "The President ... may not be prosecuted for exercising his core constitutional powers, and he is entitled, at a minimum, to a presumptive immunity from prosecution for all his official acts. That immunity applies equally to all occupants of the Oval Office, regardless of politics, policy, or party." (p. 643).

Despite the principal dissent urging the Supreme Court to "designate any course of conduct alleged in the indictment as private," Chief Justice Roberts emphasized that the Court was only ruling on what it needed to decide to dispose of the case and return it to the trial court for further findings and rulings. (p. 642)

In other words, what is private vs. official, and what is core vs. non-core, is to be determined by the facts of each case. This opens the door to future litigants based on varying fact patterns and legal theories to materially distinguish their new case from Trump v. United States.

In the present situation, there are multiple material distinctions to be made regarding the law and the facts. First and foremost, we are not talking about the criminal prosecution of the president.

Second, the proposed legal claims are to be based upon any number of Trump's actions that are overtly outside the scope of the executive powers described in Article II of the Constitution and limited by, for example, the due process requirements of the 5th and 14th Amendments to the Constitution. To wit, he cannot legally deport, without *due process*, an undocumented immigrant like Kilmar Abrego Garcia, send him to a horrific prison in El Salvador, and then falsely claim, in response to a court order, that he had no power to bring him home.

A third distinguishing feature from the Immunity case is that the proposed legal claims, individually and cumulatively, are based upon a premeditated, comprehensive, written plan (Project 2025) to weaken and destroy our democratic republic. Therefore, individual actions, understood in the larger, specific, and provable context, are not exercises of the "core powers" nor "official acts" of the president of a democratic republic.

Finally, the remedies recommended are all within the scope of established equitable relief principles. No one's liberty would be threatened, no damages would be sought, and only limited injunctive relief, if any, would be requested.

It is instructive and important to note that neither the Constitution nor any federal statute expressly provides for civil or criminal immunity for a president. See Article II, Sections I-IV. Further, the Supreme Court majority in the Immunity Case cast aside its traditional originalist/textualist interpretive modes and created brand-new, essentially unprecedented, immunity standards.

To be fair, the decision was issued in the summer of 2024, before it was crystal clear that Mr. Trump would be elected, let alone that he would aggressively move to implement Project 2025 or how intensely committed he was to retaliating against his perceived political enemies. Based upon the circumstances presented today by Mr. Trump's ongoing illegal conduct, the summer 2024 "Immunity" decision should not be a bar to the proposed litigation strategy.

State Initiated Litigation

The states are uniquely positioned to go on the offense, particularly as a team, standing together and not presenting a single target for Mr. Trump's wrath and retribution. As previously noted, the states are "parties" to the original Constitution and its many amendments. They are clearly intended beneficiaries of compliance with the Presidential Oath of Office and the Presidential Employment Contract. They therefore have standing to assert all the contract-based civil claims described above. (See Restatement (Second) of Contracts § 2 (Am. L. Inst. 1981)).

Their sovereignty, i.e., the authority of a state to govern itself, has been under attack through illegal uses of the military within state boundaries, unlawful use of State National Guard Forces in cities and states, the pending creation of a "standing National Guard quick reaction force" to be used across the country, recent efforts to take control of state election procedures and protocols, and Mr. Trump's pressure on state governors to gerrymander congressional districts to undermine the congressional power of blue states.

Importantly, in acting to enforce the plain language of the Constitution through litigation, the states have been, functionally and literally, protecting their rights under Article V to ratify (approve) any amendments to the Constitution. Yet, Mr. Trump continues to directly and repeatedly ignore the Constitution and to issue executive orders that purport to establish contrary law, and he continues to run to the Supreme Court, hoping they will overturn the lower courts.

Citizen and Non-Government Organizations (NGO's) Rights to Sue

When it comes to the rights of citizens, non-government organizations, associations, and businesses to sue for breach of the oath and the Presidential Employment Contract, they can reasonably be viewed as a "third-party beneficiary" (TPB) of that contract.

The starting point to determine TPB status is whether the contract expressly or impliedly seeks to benefit a non-contracting party. *Corbin on Contracts One Volume Edition*, Part V, Chapter 41, Section 776-777. The courts look to the language of the contract and the circumstances at the time of its creation. Id.

The primary purpose of the "Contract," i.e., the Constitution, is to empower, protect, and support the "general welfare" of the people. Individual citizens, associations, organizations, and governments that have been and continue to be systematically and directly attacked by Mr. Trump through unofficial actions in pursuit of Project 2025 goals are uniquely situated to assert TPB status under common law principles and the Constitution.

This is consistent with the general rule for "Standing" to sue in federal courts, which requires that plaintiffs have a personal stake in the outcome of the dispute—not an impact shared by all other citizens; the relief sought is causally connected to the conduct being challenged; and the alleged harm is subject to being redressed by court action.

Lujan v. Defenders of Wildlife, 504 U.S. 555, 560-61 (1992). Article III, Section 2, Clause 1.3.1 ("Cases" or "Controversies")

Not surprisingly, the issue of TPB rights in this unique factual and legal context has not been litigated, and there is a substantial, distinguishable body of case law holding that individual citizens are generally not considered third-party beneficiaries, particularly in claims for monetary damages. Pac.Gas and Elec.Co. ex rel.Brown v. United States 838 F.3d 341 (2016); Charter Bank v. Francoeur 2012-NMCA-078 (2015).

Today, however, there are thousands of people—media organizations, journalists, law firms, lawyers, universities, businesses, non-profit organizations, local, regional, and state governments, and elected representatives and former government officials, advisors, and employees that have been and continue to be directly harmed by Mr. Trump's wide-ranging, unlawful conduct. Many of them can present compelling, unique fact patterns of presidential misconduct that will support reconsideration of any potentially applicable past precedent regarding TPB status and rights.

We the People as Employers and Fraud Victims

Another possible legal avenue to end Mr. Trump's employment is to consider We the People as a co-employer of Mr. Trump, given various control factors. As previously discussed, We the People have functionally "hired" him through the general election process, pay for his salary, benefits, and retirement plan through our taxes, and we maintain control through the electoral process to not renew his contract after four years.

Through our elected representatives, We the People also have conditional, mid-contract term control over the employment contract, where our representatives can, in theory, impeach and convict Mr. Trump.

When impeachment and conviction are not possible, common law principles support We the People acting as a co-employer of Mr. Trump. And where other co-employers, like the federal government and its branches, are unable or unwilling to control and/or terminate Mr. Trump, then the other co-employer, We the People, can logically and reasonably step in and sue to rescind the employment contract. See Sandhu v. Board of Administration etc. 108 Cal.App. 5th 1048 (2025); Vernon v. State of California, 116 Cal. App. 4th 114 (2004)

There are also examples of state statutes providing for the *allocation of termination rights* (emphasis added) in co-employer situations. 40 Oklahoma Statutes, Section 600.7; Kansas Annotated Statutes, K.S.A. Section 44-1707.

Whether or not We the People step forward as third-party beneficiaries, co-employers, or both, they should definitely assert a "fraud in the inducement" claim based upon Mr. Trump's intentional, premeditated lies when he recited the Oath of Office. This is the simplest and easiest-to-prove claim against Mr. Trump and it provides a unique avenue to seek invalidation of all of his executive orders.

In this context, you'll recall that the common law remedy for this misconduct, discussed in Chapter 3, is a court determination that the contract is void, meaning it never existed. The case is quite simple: Mr. Trump lied; everyone present at the ceremony and watching it around the country acquiesced to the transfer of powers. They relied upon his promises to their detriment. There was, therefore, never an effective contract. It was void at its perceived inception.

All things considered, moving to end Mr. Trump's job, hopefully well short of four years, will, for the first time, put him on notice that he is in danger of not being able to serve a full term. Then, and only then, can we reasonably expect that he *might* begin to moderate his behaviors. And very importantly, if all of his supporters in Washington and around the country see that he is at risk of losing his position, they will be less likely to remain blindly loyal to him.

At the moment, Mr. Trump clearly has plans to remain in the position indefinitely, as he is already taking steps to control the outcome of the 2026 midterms. The more power he consolidates, the closer he comes to formally declaring himself "Supreme Ruler," "President for Life," "Chairman," "King," or some other equivalent.

The time to act is now.

The Merrick Garland-led U.S. Justice Department made a huge, historic mistake by waiting too long to proceed criminally against Mr. Trump. A similar historical error could be made by delaying the pursuit of the contract-based claims and equitable remedies detailed herein.

A Call to Action

As we are dealing here with a relatively new way for most of us to look at the Presidency, your individual help is needed. Please consider helping educate, organize, and empower your fellow citizens on these issues by actively advocating for litigation that holds Mr.

Trump accountable for the premeditated and ongoing breaches of the Oath of Office and the Presidential Employment Contract.

Appendix A lists all the blue-state governors and their contact information. Please write to the governor of your state, or, if you are in a red state, pick out a blue governor to reach out to, and advocate for the civil litigation strategy presented in this book. Even consider sending a copy of this book to the governor, with an inscribed message or highlights of pages you find essential and compelling.

Consider having a party where you get together with friends and create handwritten letters. Inscribe your books and package everything for individual or group mailing.

Appendix B contains a list of all the blue-state attorneys general, along with their contact information. Please write to them along the same lines as recommended for the governors. Also, be sure to thank them for their hard work in filing and winning many suits against Mr. Trump's ongoing, illegal actions.

Overall, the blue-state attorneys general have done exemplary work seeking to protect us from many of Mr. Trump's unlawful acts. Point out that a collective breach of contract suit by all the blue states would surely inspire many others to consider bringing their own lawsuits.

To the extent you are already connected to or associated with non-profits like the ACLU, Democracy Forward, the NAACP, Public Citizen and the Southern Poverty Law Center, and others, consider writing to them and advocating for the pursuit of breach of oath/contract litigation, and offer to donate for the specific purpose of pursuing the suggested oath litigation.

See Appendix E for an expanded list of NGOs. Also see *You Are Not Alone: Your Roadmap to Effective Political Action* by Gary Lucks, which lists 41 NGOs worthy of support.

Chapter 6

Actively Supporting the Federal Courts

Just as my father and his fellow World War II soldiers worked hard continuously to build, rebuild, and repair bridges, roads, supplies, and utility infrastructure in support of combat troops, we all need to be active on an ongoing basis in supporting the pillars and foundations of our democratic republic, which are now functionally "under siege."

All federal District Court Judges and Appellate Court justices in the federal system have taken oaths to uphold the Constitution. Rulings against the Trump administration have resulted in threats against them, their staff, and their families, and, depending upon the case, they have been expressly named and insulted in some fashion by Mr. Trump, which then led to even more threats from his most extreme supporters.

In July of this year, U.S. District Court Judge John McConnell spoke during a virtual event about the aftermath of his January 2025 ruling, which blocked one of Mr. Trump's early executive orders. He reported that his court was subsequently subjected to over 400 "vile, threatening, horrible" voicemails. One asserted he should be in prison and wished for his assassination. He has faced six death threats that were deemed credible. (The Hill.com/regulation/court-battles/5430326-trump-judges-face-threats/)

U.S. District Court Judge John Coughenour, who blocked one of Mr. Trump's first executive orders, reported that he had been "swatted." Police had come to his home with weapons in hand after someone reported he had murdered his wife. He further stated:

> "It's just been stunning to me how much damage has been done to the reputation of our judiciary because some political actors think that they can gain some advantage by attacking the independence of the judiciary and threatening the rule of law." Id.

U.S. District Court Judge Esther Salas, whose son Daniel was killed in the family home by a disgruntled lawyer in 2020, stated at a recent summer legal forum that she had tracked hundreds of threats against judges across the country this year.

One despicable threat tactic is to send pizzas in the name of her son, Daniel, to the homes of judges as an intimidation tactic, showing that the home address is known to prospective bad actors. Judge McConnell reported that he had received such a pizza.

Many of us are aware that in March of 2025, after Mr. Trump called for the impeachment of a judge who had ruled against him, Chief Justice Roberts felt it necessary to publicly state that if someone disagrees with a court decision, the proper recourse is to appeal the decision.

On June 25th, 2025, the Trump Department of Justice sued all the Judges in the U.S. District Court of Maryland—a brash, unprecedented tactic that ignored fundamental separation-of-powers principles—because it did not like the rulings being issued, primarily regarding due-process rights for undocumented residents.

Most recently a group of thirty-one retired federal court judges, appointed by presidents from both major parties, collectively submitted a "Friends of the Court Brief" to the Supreme Court in Learning Resources, Inc. v. Trump (Docket No. 24-1287) (Argued 11/5/2025) regarding the illegality of Mr. Trump levying tariffs without the consent of Congress, which expressly and exclusively holds the "power of the purse," including levying taxes.

They quoted Founder James Madison, a prominent contributor to the Federalist Papers, a collection of essays published between 1777 and 1778. Federalist No. 47 reads:

> "The accumulation of all powers, legislative, executive and judiciary, in the same hands...may justly be pronounced the very definition of tyranny."

This particular "Tariffs" case will likely be decided against the government, and the ruling will not only be a major setback for Mr. Trump but also a solid piece of evidence in a Breach of Oath lawsuit. The administration's legal position was tenuous at best. It was basically an unprecedented and arrogant overreach, as a "Tariffs" proposal could have gone to Congress for consideration. Still, Mr. Trump did not ask for approval and acted in bad faith and outside the scope of authority provided to the president by Article II (see Appendix F for the U.S. Constitution and Declaration of Independence).

A correct decision by the Supreme Court in the Tariffs case would be a boost for all the currently sitting District Court and Appellate Judges who have shown courage to stand up for and enforce the Constitution and related statutory laws against Mr. Trump's illegal actions.

Call to Action

In the meantime, please consider adding an additional "boost" by personally writing to the presiding U.S. District Court Judge and the presiding U.S. Appellate Court Justice in your area and express your gratitude, respect, and support for them and their colleagues for their commitment to honoring their oaths to uphold the Constitution. Please include a thank you to their staff.

Appendix C contains a list of the presiding district courts judges and presiding justices of the courts of appeal serving the blue and purple states, and their mailing information. Consider making signs for your next march or public gathering, thanking the judiciary for their courage in upholding the rule of law.

Further, please consider writing to the U.S. Supreme Court Justices who are in a most complicated and challenging situation. Thank you letters to the three progressive Justices and to the three possible swing votes—Roberts, Barrett, and Kavanaugh—would be in order, thanking them for taking oaths to uphold the Constitution.

Below, we will review a proposed, more detailed letter to each of the three swing votes. It is useful, however, to return briefly to the issue of how the Supreme Court Justices go about interpreting and applying the Constitution.

More on How to Interpret and Apply the Constitution

The conservative Justices, as previously mentioned, frequently rely heavily on the interpretive modes of originalism—the original meaning or intent of the words at the time they were chosen—and textualism—the ordinary meaning of the text with limited or no consideration of its intent or history—which are basically, in lay terms, methods which routinely lead to a conclusion that there is no present remedy for a problem.

The "O and T" approaches have contributed to a system unduly influenced by unlimited corporate contributions; widespread and shameless voter suppression; and anti-democratic, and often racist gerrymandering. Accordingly, we now have a miniscule, thirty to forty competitive congressional seats (out of 435), where there is a reasonable chance during each election cycle that either party could win. We also now have only seven to eight swing states in any given presidential election year, resulting in less campaigning and voter education in the other states and predictable lower voter turnout.

Without electoral competition, incumbents have little incentive to seek compromise on important and controversial public issues. They follow what can be called the "hard party line," which, in turn, fosters extreme partisanship, acrimonious debate, and no meaningful change.

Bottom line, conservative Supreme Court decisions, cumulatively over the last three to four decades, have created a governance system that is substantially paralyzed and has understandably lost the confidence of most of the American public.

To help people understand the different approaches to interpreting and applying the Constitution, the non-partisan Congressional Research Service ("CRS") has issued a report entitled "Modes of Constitutional Interpretation" (R45129) discussing eight, often overlapping but distinct interpretive methods used by the Courts: textualism, original meaning, judicial precedent, structuralism, historical practices, pragmatism, moral reasoning, and national ethos.

Different justices often use varying combinations of these modes depending upon the case. Somewhat telling indicators of recent decision-making are that morality—values such as liberty or justice—and national ethos—evolving ideas of democratic values or American identity—are often not considered, or are minimally considered, by some justices.

Pragmatism is the primary mode used by former Associate Justice Breyer, and it "evaluates the practical consequences of legal rules, often in balance with other modes." His guiding principle in this context is whether a particular decision will advance or undermine the union's viability.

It is fair to say, and many if not most constitutional scholars will tell you that, particularly with the current conservative super majority on the Court, which holds unprecedented and arguably intoxicating degrees of power—witness Justices Alito and Thomas stunning lack of judicial ethics compliance—that the justices typically use whatever modes will get them to the result they want, sometimes creating new law.

Which brings us full circle to the issue of what the Supreme Court will do with the first Presidential Breach of Oath/Employment Contract action they hear, where the bottom-line, nowhere-to-hide question is democracy or dictatorship—looking at the totality of all lawless conduct of Mr. Trump, past, present, and future.

The swing votes will predictably reason their way to the result they want, and as previously stated, it is reasonable to hope that at least two of them will join the three progressives and stand up for our democratic republic—even if it means Mr. Trump will aggressively attack them and very possibly declare he will ignore their ruling.

If Mr. Trump does ignore a favorable ruling that rescinds his employment contract or declares it void, a most important question would then become what the military will do. If the military branches follow their respective oaths of allegiance to the Constitution, not to the president, then they should no longer take orders from Mr. Trump or his Defense Secretary.

Justice Barrett was recently quoted as saying that the Court lacks the power to enforce its orders against Mr. Trump if he refuses to comply. She specifically said the Court does not have the power of the "sword" nor the power of the "purse." However, the Court does have the power of the sword if the military continues to follow Court rulings, as it is doing now regarding the use of the military in Portland, Los Angeles, Chicago, Memphis, and Washington, D.C.

Similarly, suppose the majority in Congress, with the now abdicated power of the purse, changes after the midterms and follows the employment termination order and no longer allows or supports Mr. Trump's unilateral taxing and spending practices. In that case, he will have no new money to work with going forward.

No guns, no money equals no power—eventually.

What the country needs most, right now, is a Supreme Court demonstrating its independence from Mr. Trump on the proper use of the military, fundamental balance-of-power issues like tariffs, and birthright citizenship. Otherwise, it is highly unlikely that a military leader would say no to an illegal order if he or she believes the Supreme Court is totally subservient to Mr. Trump.

Surely, a general or admiral in that position would also reasonably assume that Trump would not only try to fire them immediately but would very likely move to have them prosecuted or even summarily punished in some fashion. Again, why take the risk if there is no chance the Court would back you up?

One would have to wonder what punishment the "Secretary of War," Mr. Hegseth, would impose as appropriate punishment if there was a reasoned, good-faith refusal to obey an order. On the other side of the power equation, as previously mentioned, it is doubtful that the Supreme Court will rule against Mr. Trump on a matter related to the proper use of the military if the Supreme Court believes the military leadership is totally subservient to Mr. Trump, regardless of what it rules.

Bottom line, the country right now, one way or the other, needs to see a steady commitment by both the Supreme Court and the military to look to the Constitution of the United States, not Mr. Trump.

We All Need to Know

In this regard, it would be beneficial for someone like Fareed Zakaria, Jeffrey Goldberg, Diane Sawyer, Jimmy Kimmel, Oprah Winfrey, or other respected public figures to host, or co-host, or triple host, a nationally televised, ideally prime-time program, interviewing former Supreme Court Associate Justices Stephen Breyer and Anthony Kennedy on the proper relationship between the Supreme Court and the military

Do they think those two pillars of power now have each other's backs, so to speak?

To further explore these issues, there should be nationally televised, ideally prime-time interviews of retired military leaders like Generals Mark Milley, former Chairman of the Joint Chiefs of Staff, and John Kelly, former Marine Corps Commandant, on how the military views the Supreme Court and the related practical considerations relevant to standing up to an illegal order.

It would be very useful for everyone to know what the military leadership has been taught about how to interpret and apply the Constitution. Do they understand that the so-called "Unitary Executive Theory" is a strategy for creating an authoritarian government? Do they know that the most essential, foundational goal of the Constitution is to keep our Union together, especially with equal application of the laws to everyone? Do they understand that the interpretation modes of textualism and originalism are a major reason the country is divided today?

The suggested interviews can be immensely useful for educating everyone, including all levels of the active-duty military and members of the Supreme Court, who are likely wondering exactly what everyone else is thinking and whether they can count on each other.

As Benjamin Franklin famously said: "We must all hang together, or assuredly we shall all hang separately."

Mr. Trump Will Never Leave Voluntarily

In evaluating ongoing strategies, everyone must accept the high probability that Mr. Trump will never voluntarily leave the Office of the President unless, perhaps, it becomes clear that his health will not allow him to function in any reliable or meaningful manner. We know he relishes and emotionally needs the attention and power that he wields; that by all appearances he is enriching himself and his family to the tune of billions of dollars; and he does not want to lose his presidential immunity.

In this regard, federal charges related to January 6th could be reinstated if they are eventually adjudicated to constitute capital offenses. Such offenses have no Statute of Limitations. (18 USC Section 3281)

There are also a number of "fake elector" prosecutions still pending in some of the swing states, which could also present problems for Mr. Trump when he is out of office.

And then, with all the "transactions" he has been pursuing nationally and internationally, it is possible he will have committed any number of financial crimes that would predictably be adjudicated as outside the scope of his official duties. In this regard, Trump biographer Michael Wolff has opined that Mr. Trump will do whatever it takes to stay in power:

> "The problem…is that an authoritarian breaks so many rules and makes so many enemies that in order to avoid retribution, he has to stay in power." (As reported in "…A Never-Ending Presidency," by Katie Francis, Daily Beast, 10/19/25)

Bottom line: Mr. Trump will not stop until he is stopped. And the country needs to get on with removing him from the presidency.

Draft Letter to Supreme Court Justices

In terms of more immediate action, here is a proposed letter for specific Supreme Court Justices on the subject of following their oath and standing up for our Constitutional order. (See Appendix C Federal Courts for address).

Dear Chief Justice Roberts and Associate Justices Kavanaugh and Barrett:

Thank you for taking an oath to uphold the Constitution of the United States of America. Thank you for standing up for our democratic republic and the rule of law.

As frequent, if not regular, members of the voting conservative majority on the Court, you now hold positions of unprecedented power and immense, historic responsibility to our collective ancestors, to democratic governments around the world, and to future generations.

And as you well know, such immense power has a natural tendency to corrupt the perspective and functional values of those who hold it, and absolute power tends to corrupt absolutely. We are seeing this human frailty play out every day with Mr. Trump.

All of us will someday pass on and perhaps meet the God that you swore to in taking your oath. Still, you, as members of the Supreme Court, will be remembered for how you choose in each case between democracy and authoritarianism, and whether you helped or hindered—or even stopped—a descent into a state of conflict that Americans have not seen for over one hundred and sixty years.

You will likely be remembered by real history as true American heroes or as individuals held in the same regard as Benedict Arnold or even Joseph McCarthy.

We know that when you issued the Trump v. U.S. decision in the summer of 2024, most of you did not fully anticipate all that Donald Trump might do if he returned to the presidency. And now that everyone sees what he has done, you can see how your immunity decision and related "Unitary Executive" decisions have facilitated the rise of an authoritarian leader who is well on the way to permanently destroying our democracy.

And that same leader is now supported by an array of billionaire oligarchs who are fully invested in him remaining in power through expanded control of the free press, the facilitation of relentless lies and propaganda, and the functional, outright purchase of seats in Congress because we have no meaningful limits on campaign contributions.

As Mr. Trump clearly intends to do everything in his power to ensure he never loses an election again, he is actively conspiring with cooperative red states to rig the midterms to make sure that majorities in Congress will always support him.

Your decisions are being watched closely by all those in power across the political spectrum, including the military. It appears, for the time being, that the military branches are respecting the Courts' decisions on the use of the military against American citizens. Apparently, for the time being, they would likely refuse to take orders to fire on American citizens.

But that could change. The military needs to see now that the Supreme Court is not entirely subservient to Mr. Trump; otherwise, it is left to stand alone against him when truly difficult choices present themselves. Their question in the face of an illegal order would be whether the Courts would back up them up? If the refusal would be futile, why take that risk?

Alternatively stated, and with due respect to Justice Barrett, you do hold the power of the sword if you hold the respect and allegiance of the military. You do have the power of the purse if Congress sees you stand up to Mr. Trump's illegal appropriation of that power and decides to follow balance of powers principles.

It is logical that the daily goal of the court is to survive Mr. Trump, and to avoid truly "poking the bear." You rightfully do not want him to declare complete independence from the Judiciary.

However, every day, with the rapid expansion of his personal paramilitary force (ICE) and the continuing purges of generals and admirals deemed insufficiently loyal, he seems to be moving in that direction. I implore you to stand up to him, sooner than later, with a strongly worded opinion on the proper use of the military and with a clear message to the military, in some form, that you have its back if the need arises to refuse an illegal order.

Please make us proud to be Americans.

Chapter 7

Supporting Our Military Through Our Veterans

Mr. Trump's recent unprecedented, and highly divisive political speech before the entire leadership of the U.S. Military was clearly inappropriate on many levels. Most importantly, the generals and admirals proudly consider themselves non-political, and it was a massive insult to them to publicly implore them to functionally become a military arm of the Trump political machine.

At the same time, it can be said that Mr. Trump did us all a favor in publicly admitting his goal of using the military to threaten, oppress, and even shoot his domestic opponents. This was a stunning breach of his Oath of Office. Admonishing the military to be prepared to fight American citizens—"the enemy within"—was a blatant betrayal and material breach of his oath. And it was done amid a background of him already actively working to insert the military into Democratic cities to illegally be used as law enforcement against citizens in opposition to him and his policies.

Out of respect for the non-partisan pride of our military leadership, a direct letter-writing campaign thanking them for taking their oaths to uphold the Constitution would not be appropriate. We do not want anyone in the military to construe our efforts as an improper attempt to exert political influence.

What we can and should do is to support an unprecedented, nationwide effort to thank our 18 million military veterans for taking oaths to uphold the Constitution and for their service to our country. Additionally, we should join forces with those veterans who feel strongly that military troops, including the State National Guard, should not be used against civilians except in the direst circumstances where civil law enforcement is clearly unable to stop actual violence.

Additional common ground includes objecting to the military preparing for and in some cases already fighting a non-congressionally authorized war against Venezuela, and the Trump Administration cutting Veterans benefits while spending money on a ballroom and providing a $20 billion bailout to Argentina.

Many veterans, no doubt, are aware of Trump's draft dodger status, his insults to fallen American soldiers buried in France, and the fact that he is constantly lying about something.

Overall, we have a lot in common with our veterans, who are active and vibrant members of our society and often run their own businesses and serve as employers. We need to consider them allies in our fight against the Trump administration's lawlessness. Plus, we can count on veterans knowing many people in the active military.

We also need to recognize that the general public and far too many elected representatives have been remiss for decades in not prioritizing the very best post-service support and health care for our veterans, and in not paying the enlisted men and women livable salaries while they are serving.

I have lived in San Diego County for almost forty years, and every holiday season, there are drives for food and toys for active-duty military families. The necessity for that has been an ongoing national disgrace, reflective of, among other things, the public's failure to appreciate the valiant, essential role of our military in taking and abiding by their Constitutional Oath, including, most importantly, putting their lives on the line to protect our freedoms.

Now is the time to accomplish three primary, complementary, and essential goals. First, we need to wholeheartedly thank our veterans for taking their oaths and for their service. We also need to let our elected representatives know that post-service benefits need not only to be fully restored but amply enhanced. Lastly, we need to advocate for much higher pay and benefits for those now serving.

Our country's failure to proudly and adequately compensate our active military and our veterans reflects a nation that has lost contact with its roots and has largely forgotten those who have sacrificed over the last 250 years to protect our nation.

There can be no debate or doubt that, in the world we live in today, we need a strong military to keep the peace and a military firmly committed to upholding our Constitution, with proud allegiance to the rule of law and not the rule of men.

In addition to advocating to our elected representatives, we can support our veterans by calling or writing to anyone we know, directly or indirectly, who has served and thanking them for their service. Many, if not most, of the individuals who have signed up with a branch of the Armed Services or the National Guard have done so out of a sense of duty and a commitment to serve their fellow Americans and our country. I know, for example, how proud my father was to have served his country in World War II.

Feel free to ask any veteran you know about how that service positively influenced their volunteering today.

You can provide further reciprocal service to them by supporting national and/or local veteran groups—and active military support non-profit organizations—by regularly donating and/or participating in Veterans Day and Memorial Day events. There are, for example, over 170 national military cemeteries across the country where we can pay our respects to service members buried there.

Before visiting, be sure to check the cemetery website for visiting days and hours, as well as protocols regarding attire and conduct. Appendix D lists veterans' support organizations and active-duty military support organizations.

Law Enforcement Members, Civil Servants, Congressional Representatives, and Attorneys

Moving forward, be sure to keep in mind that civilian law enforcement officers, civil servants at all levels of government, your congressional representative, your U.S. senator, and attorneys have all taken an oath to uphold the Constitution. If you know someone in one of these roles, please be on the lookout for opportunities to thank them for their commitment and public service. Consider sending letters to your congressional representative and your U.S. senator, thanking them for taking their oath and encouraging them to support the American Oath Project.

On the subject of local law enforcement, I would like to mention that at the end of the recent "No Kings II March" in downtown San Diego on October 18th, 2025, I made a point of walking up to six different police SUV's, each with two officers, that had been slowly and at a respectful distance, bringing up the rear of the march to mark the end of the event and the reopening of the street behind them.

I looked through the open side windows and said to the occupants of each vehicle, "Thank you for facilitating an orderly and peaceful march." They were all smiles.

And one of them even thanked me.

Chapter 8

Educating the Voters and Using The News Cycle

If there were only one Breach of Employment Contract suit filed, and there should be dozens, if not hundreds, by different plaintiffs with a variety of priority wrongs against them, the most powerful would be on behalf of all the blue states that have been litigating since the beginning of Trump 2.0. They can all stand together against the probable furious responses of Mr. Trump and his lawyers—all paid for by your tax dollars.

When an initial lawsuit is filed, federal courts require early, detailed discovery plans that identify deposition witnesses and schedules, the documents to be obtained, and the timing for any motions to be brought to the court for resolution. This plan is basically a schedule for the lawyers to making best efforts to follow.

That discovery plan can be considered a parallel press release/press conference game plan, in which discovery and motion events can be previewed, disclosed, and used to set up the next mini drama to unfold. In this regard, think of the way the January 6th congressional hearings kept everyone's interest with many high-profile witnesses being called to testify every week for a period of months.

The Trump administration will first and foremost seek to dismiss the litigation on several grounds. Most fundamentally, they will argue that there is no precedent and the legal theory is not expressly authorized in the Constitution. Assuming the lawsuit is not dismissed, then the defense will seek to delay everything, including asserting immunity for Mr. Trump and others

When witnesses finally sit for deposition, a number of them will possibly plead the 5th Amendment. These actions and everything else should be placed before the public, and everyone should anticipate that Mr. Trump, from time to time, will be watching and likely commenting on his social media page, with content that could be used against him.

Co-benefits of keeping everything significant about the ongoing litigation in the press include distracting those doing Mr. Trump's bidding and reminding them that they may eventually face accountability. Right now, and as previously mentioned, it is fair to say that most of those subordinates feel they are untouchable, and we need to do our best to disabuse them of that notion.

Every other case filed by plaintiffs seeking Mr. Trump's departure should follow a similar game plan: aggressive, pervasive press interaction.

There could be limited, common-interest groups of states that are particularly affected and concerned with specific types of misconduct, serving as plaintiffs. For instance, most southern border states face unique problems related to immigration enforcement, due process rights, and birthright citizenship. Northern states around the Great Lakes have been hit hard with negative impacts on labor and union rights, which the 1st Amendment and the Commerce Clause in the Constitution protect.

Because the list of unconstitutional acts is extensive and continues to grow, there are many different combinations of plaintiffs that could file their own lawsuits in various parts of the country. When these are to be filed, the entire country needs to be notified, and everyone needs to know what is happening with the other suits.

Not only do we want to keep the citizenry informed, but we also need to remind the court system, the military, the National Guard, local law enforcement, and civil servants that there is a chance Mr. Trump may not be around for his entire term.

And keep in mind, in the future, every illegal act by Mr. Trump would be additional evidence in support of the basic proposition that he has not and will never abide by his oath of office. It is therefore possible that he could reconsider some of his next steps.

Mr. Trump will predictably "fight like hell" to avoid testifying, and the courts may very well say he does not have to show up for deposition. One possible, court-ordered alternative would be for him to answer written questions. And the chances of him then taking the 5th Amendment, as he has done hundreds of times already in other legal matters, are significant.

Bottom line, we don't know what Mr. Trump will do in response to the proposed litigation. He will probably help bolster the cases against him with his always very public, unpresidential, threatening, and retaliatory actions.

Recall the legal theory of "anticipatory breach." Fair questions in discovery would ask Mr. Trump about his perceptions of his future rights to pressure his vice president not to certify election results, to create a slate of electors from states he does not win in 2028, and about his future ability to seize voting machines, etc. He will either take the 5th Amendment or double down and insist he has, effectively, complete power.

Such claims would be beneficial in reaffirming the intent to destroy our democratic republic.

With this type of news in the headlines, Mr. Trump's enablers and co-conspirators could, again, have some second thoughts about how long their boss is going to be around. At some point, you could even have some "whistleblowers" stepping forward, although this is not a probability given the unprecedented climate of fear and intimidation created by Trump.

Chapter 9

Parallel State Actions

As the public and others watch these civil litigation efforts unfold, the states need to pursue multifaceted, go-on-the-offense strategies in addition to the proposed litigation efforts.

Banning Corporate Political Contributions

States should go to work passing legislation or using initiative power to 1) ban state-chartered corporations from making political donations to candidates in their states; and 2) ban out-of-state-chartered corporations from doing the same.

All domestic corporations enjoy their unique status through the grant of protections and privileges from the state in which they are chartered. The states, therefore, have the power to prohibit political contributions by those corporations.

New law in this regard promises to materially reduce the flow of corporate dollars supporting, directly or indirectly, the Trump Administration and its allies in Congress and elsewhere. It will help put the malignant, cancerous effects of the "Citizens United" Supreme Court case into remission, which equated dollar expenditures with free speech and determined that corporations were, effectively, people, with 1st Amendment rights to make political contributions.

Tom Moore, a Senior Fellow for Democracy Policy at the Center for American Progress, has reported that an initiative prohibiting corporate political contributions is currently "moving toward the state's 2026 ballot" in Montana. He summed up the opportunity for other states in a recent *USA Today* opinion piece:

> "Americans across the political spectrum overwhelmingly oppose Citizens United and want to rid our political system of corporate and dark money. Through their states, they have the power to end it—not someday, not via federal constitutional amendment or some miracle at the Supreme Court—but now." (9/17/2025)

Any new laws on this front must include effective monitoring and enforcement mechanisms to ensure that corporations do not launder or use other avoidance/channeling methods to funnel money to candidates and office holders. The laws need to expressly preclude alleged charitable donations to partisan entities parading as non-profits.

Unfair Competition Laws

California can provide critical leadership by amending its current "Unfair Competition Law" (Business and Professions Code Section 17200 et al.) to allow enforcement by private citizens and public interest groups with attorney-fee recovery rights against so-called news organizations engaging in systematic, for-profit, fraudulent business practices.

There needs to be meaningful guardrails around companies that systematically and intentionally lie, filter, distort, and obscure the truth as part of a daily business model designed to anger and scare viewers for profit.

Opponents will vigorously claim interference with their 1st Amendment rights, but the scope, depth, and pervasiveness of misinformation and the related, deceptive "information bubbles" separating Americans and chilling meaningful public discourse are such a critical, ongoing problem that new laws need to be adopted to create meaningful safeguards.

Yes, any new laws will be tested in the courts, but there are major factual and solid public policy reasons to distinguish past case law, to establish standards to protect the public's mental health, and to protect the 1st Amendment rights of the *recipients* of the lies. Without the facts, citizens cannot meaningfully debate the issues or cast an informed vote. Indeed, the falsehoods they are told are often designed to discourage people from voting at all.

One way to help avoid a successful 1st Amendment challenge in the context of Unfair Competition Laws is to include specific language prohibiting elder abuse through the deceitful manipulation of emotions. Many of us know that older people are often more easily persuaded and emotionally vulnerable. Add this to the fact that most conservative news outlets typically appeal to the over-65 viewer, and you have a major society-wide problem.

These senior citizens are literally targeted and manipulated for profit, and it is fundamentally unfair and even inhumane for an entire society to turn a blind eye to this process or to conclude there is nothing to be done about it. Further, the continuing efforts to consolidate media ownership with Trump-supporting billionaires and large corporations make it even more urgent that we rethink and update our 1st Amendment laws.

In this regard, Mr. Trump's apparent ongoing efforts to have TikTok purchased by his billionaire friends suggest a possible future in which new algorithms by design seek to move tens of millions of subscribers into a deceptive, conservative information bubble. We can be sure Mr. Trump's well-known, full-embrace of AI technology is very much related to his drive to rewrite history, deny science, and control the flow of information to all American citizens.

Discipline for Unethical Lawyers

Another state-level strategy should include the prompt pursuit of disciplinary actions against lawyers working for Trump—whether privately or through federal departments/agencies—who have been making misrepresentations to the courts, pursuing meritless, politically vindictive lawsuits, and otherwise violating professional ethical standards.

Concerns about professional discipline or the loss of a law license should help deter future misconduct by extreme partisans and unethical lawyers working for Mr. Trump. To be clear, the DOJ is still staffed with large numbers of honest, hard-working, non-partisan, and highly ethical lawyers. Many of their colleagues, tragically, have been forced to resign or have been fired and replaced with Trump loyalists.

All lawyers who practice in federal courts need to be admitted to a State Bar in at least one state. Therefore, any Trump lawyers practicing in federal courts need to be in good standing with their respective state bar associations. And Mr. Trump's pardon power does not extend to state law licensing requirements.

In a recent opinion piece in the *Los Angeles Times*, Ethics Law Professor David Schultz wrote that:

> "[A] functioning democracy requires the legal profession to uphold higher standards of truth, candor and fairness. Attorneys cannot hide behind their clients' political power or use their licenses as shields for misconduct. Their duty is to the rule of law itself, not to a particular office holder. It is a reminder that a powerful tool to curb the Trump administration's legal excesses has been underused. State Boards should go after the attorneys who are enabling Trump's behavior." (11/5/2025)

Consistent with this advice, The Campaign for Accountability (CAP), a non-profit ethics watchdog group in Washington D.C., has recently approached the state bar associations in Virginia and in Florida, asking them to investigate DOJ attorney Lindsay Halligan and her decisions to indict Trump "enemies" when career prosecutors in the DOJ previously concluded there was insufficient evidence to indict.

We can assume that if those bar associations open the requested inquiries, future DOJ indictment decisions will consider, somewhat more carefully, indicting someone just because Mr. Trump wants them charged.

Interstate Mediation Efforts

In addition to these going-on-the-offense options, the states should consider pursuing a multi-state mediation process. Mediation involves bringing individuals or entities with a dispute together and, with the assistance of a mediator, helping them resolve the conflict. Similar efforts are made every day across the United States, sometimes to head off potential litigation, sometimes when the parties want to settle a pending lawsuit.

Mediations are usually successful when the parties get together and work in good faith to find common ground. The process requires a commitment to confidentiality, which includes a signed agreement to that effect. Where there is no resolution or settlement, what was said is inadmissible in court and not to be released to the public.

Given the divisions in Washington these days, and particularly the overbearing occupant of the White House, the states should consider having a confidential mediation gathering to talk about pressing state issues like 1) deployment of one state's national guard into another, particularly when one state is a red state and the other is blue; 2) federal immigration enforcement, including prohibiting masked ICE agents and jointly defining the appropriate roles of local law enforcement; and 3) the future of federal disaster relief as Mr. Trump apparently wants to turn the responsibility over to the individual states which is, by the way, a terrible idea.

There is common ground amongst the states on these issues and many other matters but the oppressive political climate strongly discourages problem solving dialogue. What would happen if, after Mr. Trump exploded upon hearing about a mediation gathering, several red, blue, and purple states got together to discuss these issues confidentially? Then they subsequently issued a proposal, for example, that a National Guard deployment in another state should occur only after a designated monitor or monitoring team agrees that law enforcement could not handle a given situation.

This would address only part of the problems associated with National Guard troops being nationalized and wrongfully deployed, but it could be a helpful first step. There is no good reason for any state to continue to sit back and let Mr. Trump decide what should be done when he is not concerned at all about what is best for the National Guard members and the citizens of both the sending and receiving states.

Our National Guard and our military are now being overtly used as pawns in Mr. Trump's grand Project 2025 plan. A coalition of red, blue, and purple states standing together and making reasonable suggestions for priorities and processes could put real pressure on Mr. Trump to reconsider his actions or at least give the judges on the front lines some good ideas for fashioning orders in a litigation setting.

What we see day to day is Mr. Trump slugging it out with the blue states in the press and in the courts, with him still basically free to unilaterally decide where and when to send more troops into additional cities, impacting more families and their communities in so many negative ways.

If there were a gathering of say, twenty-one governors—or, initially, their representatives—with maybe seven "brave souls" from red states, seven "cautious souls" from swing states, and seven "hopeful souls" from blue states, and they participated in good faith in the confidential process, imagine the impact of a resulting consensus position on these most challenging issues.

An of example a "brave soul" candidate from a red state would be the Governor of Nebraska, who recently won the Republican primary and is seeking another term despite not being backed by Mr. Trump. There are currently thirty-one states classified as red based on the results of the 2024 presidential election, and it seems likely that at least six other brave souls would wish to participate.

Keep in mind that red states are very focused on states' rights, and the proposed mediation process is an exercise in states working together, with no representative of the federal government present, to resolve a problem created by the federal government. There is clearly room for finding common ground, but people first need to really talk to one another.

Process-wise, the group could initially plan a series of three one-day meetings over three weeks. Time, of course, is of the essence as the latest news is that Mr. Trump wants 20,000 National Guard troops to be specially trained and ready for rapid deployment by the first month of 2026.

Ideally, the mediation participants would be identified over the 2025-26 wintertime frame and the actual mediation dates set for early summer. The group organizers could begin their first public outreach by asking Mr. Trump to defer any further troop deployments until the states have a chance to meet.

Mr. Trump would probably reject the request, but any number of reactions could occur in different places, including in the courts where other deployment cases may be pending. Remember, Mr. Trump has plans to deploy troops to many other states, so there could be a dozen or more lawsuits over deployment to other blue states by early 2026.

In this regard, it is common for judges to "stay"—or hold—further court proceedings when outside events might influence the need for a definitive legal ruling. If there was an expectation of a creative and effective proposed solution to a deployment-related dispute, a judge or judges could decide to hold everything in abeyance by freezing or continuing to freeze a particular deployment.

The mediation process and goals could also be seen by National Guard leadership as a basis for encouraging the president to wait and see what the states come up with. This and many other responses would all result in a needed disruption of the status quo, in which Mr. Trump does what he wants and people go to court to stop him. He needs to hear regularly from other people, including allies, that there are different ways to do things. The more people dare to debate him, even lightly, the more others are encouraged to do the same.

Bottom line: the states should go on the *offensive* with a civil, peaceful mediation! We need to keep shaking things up!

Eventually, consensus-based recommendations from the mediation participants would likely have the attention of all the folks in Washington and around the country. Further, Mr. Trump's expected refusal to go along with reasonable suggestions would not help his approval ratings. And harkening back to our breach of oath/contract strategy, refusal to follow reasonable suggestions from a governors' mediation group would be more evidence of Mr. Trump's bad faith.

Judges handling other deployment cases could even order the parties to go to a settlement conference and consider the publicly available mediation panel recommendations as a starting point for a global case settlement.

Maybe, for example, a state and a city could agree to a limited deployment based on court-ordered limits on where the troops are physically located, and there are strict, court-backed orders for them to stay at least a half mile away from all polling places during voting periods.

Also, the parties could agree that the troops are not to seize voting machines at any time without a valid court order. A settlement agreement would logically include a process for verification, ensuring that all deployed troops are fully informed of the restrictions on their movements and actions. In the event they receive a counter order, a monitor will be on hand as a direct connection to the judge for them to seek guidance. The court order would also direct commanding officers to strictly respect any requests for legal advice from anyone under their command.

If I were representing the local police or the state in this setting, I would recommend that, wherever troops are deployed, there be nearby reserve rapid-response local law enforcement personnel available to respond promptly to any backup requests. This will make it more difficult for Trump to claim that local police cannot handle a particular street conflict.

The court-ordered settlement should clearly specify the type of evidence the administration must present to the court to obtain the troops' release from deployment restrictions.

This list of theoretical settlement terms demonstrates that it could be a good strategy to meet the administration halfway on some issues rather than forcing the court to make a complete determination on the merits in every case. In this regard, what would happen if out of twelve future deployment cases, half were settled along these lines, based upon the specific needs of the particular city or state? The model, so to speak, could become a guide, but not necessarily a blueprint, for future court orders in the more contentious jurisdictions.

And among the many benefits of a settlement negotiation and a settlement along the lines discussed would be the national guard folks seeing how a dynamic separation-of-powers process works, where everyone agrees that the courts, not Mr. Trump, will be the final decision-maker on what is legal or not.

Additional Mediation Process Considerations

To provide political cover for all mediation participants, they need to agree in advance that the group will not put forward any positions unless everyone agrees. And it may turn out there are no agreements whatsoever, but I believe this is unlikely if the process is pursued diligently by all participants.

Everyone will probably learn something new about others' real views and actually find some common ground on many of the underlying issues. They will also have demonstrated to each other the value of civility in a democratic process and set a very valuable example for the rest of the country.

Choosing the best-qualified mediator will be important, and I would suggest three, one selected by each group of seven. The mediator panel members can take turns chairing the meetings. The mediator chairs should be experienced, as apolitical as possible, and empowered to remind people in the meetings that they are there to find common ground, not to repeat political talking points.

Alternatively stated, participants will not be there to represent their political party but to discuss good public policy for their states.

A different spokesperson for the whole group should be chosen to address the media after each session. For efficiency and predictability, and depending in part on where all the state representatives will be traveling from, the meetings would take place in one participating state, in or closest to the middle of the country.

The start of each meeting should include reciting the Pledge of Allegiance and a brief custom oath to maintain confidentiality and civility. This will help set a positive tone. And it really works.

Most of the specific process details I have suggested here can be readily adjusted. There is no magic in the number twenty-one states, but preliminarily, it is a reasonable given the need for enough time for people to express opinions. We are, after all, talking about politicians.

Please reach out to your governor and your attorneys general in support of this process and ask them to get busy organizing!

Chapter 10

A Symbol for A Mass Movement

On a near-daily basis, Mr. Trump and his administration are busy sowing misinformation, prejudice, fear, and anger with the primary goal of dividing and conquering our democratic republic. He serves as an inspiration for would-be and actual authoritarian leaders around the world.

Mr. Trump has made conflict and psychological warfare, for those of us paying attention, a regular and relentless part of our daily lives—on, it seems, nearly every level of our existence. As an aggressive denier of climate change, Mr. Trump is literally at war with the ecology of the planet.

He is directly or indirectly at war with other countries, religions, ethnic groups, and cultures. Witness Ukraine, Gaza, Venezuela, and, more broadly, with immigrants from all over the world. He is at war with the Democratic Party, the Green Party, "the enemy within"—as stated in his recent, unprecedented gathering of generals and admirals—and every other group and individual that does not support his extreme nationalist agenda.

Mr. Trump is at war with facts, history, science, and centuries of accumulated human knowledge. He literally tells blatant lies and half-truths nearly every day. He materially breaches the 1st Amendment almost daily by threatening and attacking in various ways universities, law firms, the free press, and political opponents.

Mr. Trump and his billionaire friends are busy working to buy and/or consolidate control over major independent news sources and social media companies with the apparent goals of depriving citizens of a meaningful basis upon which to exercise 1st Amendment rights.

Mr. Trump's ICE has spent over $70,000,000.00 so far in 2025 on firearms, tear gas, and guided missiles, moving toward becoming a massive personal military force, available to be used against U.S. citizens, not just immigrants.

In September of this year, ICE entered into $1.4 billion in surveillance technology contracts, which will support a "Big Brother" system where the government is in a war setting with all Americans, not just immigrants, who will be monitored through social media and other avenues of communication.

In light of these and many, many more unprecedented, coordinated, and anti-democracy actions, what symbol or symbols can best convey a firm response from Americans coming together in a thoughtful, non-partisan, unifying movement to fight back against Mr. Trump's authoritarian plans?

"The OATH PEACE SYMBOL"

To begin our "tour" for understanding the symbols and words within this circle, please consider the following from the Declaration of Independence:

> "We hold these truths to be self-evident, that all men are created equal, that they are endowed by their Creator with certain unalienable Rights, that among these are Life, Liberty and the pursuit of Happiness. —That to secure these rights,

Governments are instituted among Men, deriving their just powers from the consent of the governed …"

Also known as We the People.

And from the Constitution:

"WE THE PEOPLE of the United States, in order to form a more perfect union, establish justice, insure domestic tranquility, provide for the common defense, promote the general welfare, and secure the blessings of liberty to ourselves and our posterity, do ordain and establish this Constitution for the United States of America."

The American Flag's colors: red stands for valor and bravery, white represents purity and innocence, and blue symbolizes vigilance, perseverance, and justice. The thirteen stripes and thirteen stars represent the original thirteen colonies that declared independence from England in 1776.

The Flag waves as a tribute to many things, but perhaps most importantly to our patriotic and heroic American ancestors and contemporaries.

The dove is traditionally considered a messenger of peace and harmony, and a harbinger of new beginnings and hope. Some traditions view it as a messenger from loved ones who have passed.

The Bald Eagle, our national bird, symbolizes freedom, independence, and strength. In Native American culture, it is seen as a messenger between earth and sky and to the "Great Spirit."

The Statue of Liberty represents a nation that has historically welcomed and benefited greatly from immigrants from all over the world. Today, it is a reminder that we need to find our way back to treating all immigrants with respect and compassion, and to recognize their ongoing contributions to our society and our economy.

The raised right hand in this illustration is intended to be viewed as a dual symbol. First, the raised hand and the torch have always symbolized enlightenment and freedom. Today, it is respectfully suggested that we also view it as a hand raised in taking an oath to uphold the Constitution.

The inclusion of the words Life • Liberty • Happiness symbolizes the "American Dream," where everyone has the opportunity to work hard and achieve success and a better life. The word "Oath" is a tribute to all those, past and present, who have taken an oath to uphold the Constitution, many of whom have given their "last full measure of devotion." "We the People" reflects the Constitution's inspired and revolutionary commitment to a balance of powers in the structure and operation of our democratic republic, as well as to equal protection of the laws for everyone.

Importantly, the word "Democracy" is supported on its right by "Truth" and on the left by "Equality." It is, figuratively speaking, "embraced" by the Constitution and the Declaration of Independence for a full 360 degrees.

And the American Flag has "its back."

The "Bill of Rights" is the name of the first ten amendments to the Constitution, including the 9th Amendment, which provides that the "enumeration of certain rights" shall not be used to "deny" others retained by the people, and the 10th Amendment, which provides that the state powers not explicitly addressed in the Constitution are reserved to states.

And most Americans are familiar in general with the 1st Amendment of the Bill of Rights, but here is the specific language which everyone should memorize:

> "Congress shall make no law respecting an establishment of religion or prohibiting the free exercise thereof; or abridging the freedom of speech, or of the press, or the right of the people to peaceably assemble, and to petition the government for redress of grievances." U.S. Const. amend. 1

This language, for various reasons, reminds me of our "Pledge of Allegiance," by which these days I take comfort in reciting from time to time, with my right hand over my heart.

> "I pledge allegiance to the Flag of the United States of America, and to the Republic for which it stands, one Nation, under God, indivisible, with liberty and justice for all." 4 U.S.C. § 4

Moving forward, to help hold these principles in our hearts and minds, we might consider a commitment to each other to wear, in public, in some fashion, the suggested Oath Peace Symbol or a traditional peace symbol every day until the Trump nightmare is over. Put the symbol on hats, pins, shirts, jewelry, armbands, COVID masks, water bottles, signs and flags, stationery, email source recitals, vehicles, and even on an arm or ankle in the form of a temporary (or not) tattoo!

Maybe keep a modest supply of handouts for friends, family, and new friends. And how about a symbol on our scarves or a collar on our pets when they are out in public? Every day, we can be a source of inspiration for each other. We don't need to wait for the next march or demonstration to share and absorb the commitment, energy, and goodwill of our fellow citizens. Every day, our Oath Peace Symbol can serve as an invitation for people we don't know to ask us why we are wearing it and what it means.

On October 18th, 2025, seven million people showed up in their communities and marched on "No Kings II Day." In downtown San Diego, where I participated, the crowd appeared to be double the size of the group that showed up in June, and, indeed, crowds were larger around the country.

To help keep this promising momentum going, let's have millions of people every day wearing the Oath Peace Symbol in compelling and inspiring contrast to the war that Mr. Trump is waging against everyone, everywhere.

And who, by the way, can comfortably say they are against peace?

In the future, when we are at gatherings or in the streets in demonstrations or marches, "The OATH PEACE SYMBOL" will directly remind everyone there with guns that we are committed to non-threatening, civil, and peaceful expression of our 1st Amendment rights. It will also speak powerfully to every judge who may be asked to decide whether the Trump administration was "untethered" from the facts in describing a threat of violence from people wearing peace symbols.

And with some hesitation, I will also observe with a sad smile that if you were ever assaulted by an ICE agent or other armed individual, it would be helpful for your civil assault and battery case to place in evidence that you were wearing an Oath Peace Symbol.

And on the subject of other appropriate symbols, everyone might also consider wearing a flower image when out in public. I have, for example, a small, three-quarter-inch pin with a picture of a California poppy—my state's flower. I'm thinking I'm wearing that, too, for future gatherings.

Wearing a state flower or a picture of one could, among other impacts, make an additional, mild, positive impression on your local law enforcement members and/or your State National Guard should you by chance find yourself in their company. A tattoo of the flower may be a bridge too far for me personally, but I will think about an Oath PEACE Symbol tattoo.

And keep in mind, for the unpredictable future, we may find ourselves at a gathering and getting very mad about the people standing there with guns and the audacity of those who ordered them to be there. In those settings, our displayed symbols can serve to remind us and others that we must remain fully committed to peaceful protests, whether demonstrations, marches, or other group activities.

Trump clearly wants violence that he can cast as being out of the control of local law enforcement. Every time you wear the Oath Peace Symbol, remind yourself, perhaps along with a smile, that you are doing precisely the opposite of what he wants.

And there may come a time for strategic civil disobedience. For now, however, we want to find common ground with everyone, including the police, the National Guard troops, and active-duty military, to name a few. Blocking a door, a road, or an officer of the law can easily lead to assaults and batteries, and potential group violence coming from both directions. Now is not the time, particularly when we are approaching several key decisions by the Supreme Court on the use of the military, tariffs, and birthright citizenship, for anything other than peaceful protest.

The rulings in these Supreme Court cases will tell us a great deal about whether the Court is willing to meaningfully restrain Mr. Trump on at least some of the most critical abuses of power. If we win in some fashion on these and other matters, and Trump follows the court orders—which is a big if—civil disobedience may not ever become necessary.

In the meantime, we also need to acknowledge and support all those individuals, groups, organizations, and governments who are litigating to stop hundreds of Mr. Trump's illegal orders and actions, and who we want to initiate Breach of Oath-centered contract litigation.

Chapter 11

Educating Ourselves and Joining Together

With all this in mind, we must strive to better educate ourselves and others about the fundamental content of our Constitution. The document is the oldest and shortest Constitution in the world, consisting of only 4,400 words, or about fifteen pages. This includes the Preamble, the Seven Articles, and the 27 Amendments.

Reading 300 words per minute, it will take you 14.7 minutes.

I can see any number of creative bumper stickers related to this subject. Perhaps something straightforward like "14.7 minutes" or "Our 14.7 minutes" or "Build Back with 14.7 minutes" or even something mildly humorous like "What's the best use of 14.7 minutes? Read the Constitution!"

There is a variety of compact pamphlet editions of the Constitution available online, and one in particular I would recommend is *U.S. Constitution Rhymes: A Fun and Easy Way to Learn and Love the Constitution*, by Debbi S. Rollo.

With this book, you could organize a "Constitution Coffee" gathering and take turns reading the Rhymes above. Or, better yet, find some family time to introduce your kids and/or grandkids to the content.

There is a certain natural rhythm to the flow and meaning of the original wording. (See Appendix F) The Rhymes, however, help with remembering the specific content. And they are fun candidates for collective recitation during marches, demonstrations, and other events in support of our democratic republic.

If you have, as many of us do, a family member, friend, or neighbor with whom you've had some significant "political disagreement," you may consider reaching out to them and expressing interest in hearing their views on the U.S. Constitution. Ideally, try to get together in person, but if on the phone or Zoom, be the very best listener to everything they have to say.

Plan to ask them about any ancestors or friends who have served in the military or are currently serving, and whether they are aware that those folks have all taken oaths to uphold the Constitution. Do make it clear sooner than later that you do not want to talk about any particular political figure. If they're going to talk about someone, listen carefully and avoid any debate about that person, whoever it may be.

In a functioning democracy, everyone needs to be seen and heard. And everyone needs to be treated politely and respectfully. We need to make civility a cornerstone of a renewed American culture and society.

The Institute for Civility defines the word as follows:

"Civility is claiming and caring for one's identity, needs, and beliefs without degrading someone else's in the process."
Cassandra Dahnke & Tomas Spath, What Is Civility?, Inst. for Civility,
https://www.instituteforcivility.org/who-we-are/what-is-civility/.

Wikipedia.org defines it as "orderly behavior and politeness" and comments that "it has been described as a skill of discussing topics that are important to one with others who disagree and do so without any serious falling out."

By investing time and energy in reading our Constitution and sharing and discussing it with others, we will be better prepared to stand up to the highly partisan political appointees and other proclaimed experts who cleverly interpret and misapply the Constitution for anti-democratic purposes.

Concisely stated, our Constitution is all about what's reasonable. It's just that simple. And all those who take an oath to uphold the Constitution need to always keep this principle in their mind and heart. And as good citizens of a democratic republic, we all need to move forward every day with civility and in pursuit of common ground on the challenging issues of our time.

Imagine now, if you will, standing in the company of my father's four high school classmates and with the other thirty-two young soldiers who also passed far too soon during World War II. Imagine singing together a song like "America the Beautiful" or saying the Pledge of Allegiance and smiling at them. Imagine giving each one of them a hug and telling them you will not let their sacrifices be in vain.

We are all "standing on the shoulders" of our ancestors, with a most profound obligation to future generations to rebuild for them a vibrant democratic republic. And to meet that challenge, we must all come together as one irresistible force to oppose and prevail against Mr. Trump's relentless attacks on our democracy.

In the spirit of preserving our Union, we can find inspiration in the concluding words of Thomas Paine in "Common Sense," his famous essay in 1776 advocating for Independence from the King of England:

"On these grounds, I rest the matter. *[W]herefore*, instead of gazing at each other with suspicious or doubtful curiosity, let each of us hold out to his neighbor the hearty hand of friendship, and unite in drawing a line, which, like an act of oblivion, shall bury in forgetfulness every former dissension. Let the names of Whig [conservatives] and Tory [liberals] be extinct; and let none other be heard among us, than those of a good citizen, an open and resolute friend, and a virtuous supporter of the rights of mankind, and of the free and independent States of America."

(bracket content added)

Afterword

As this book is going to press, the latest, major, daily "Trump" news is that several members of Congress with military or intelligence backgrounds have publicly urged active-duty military members to disobey illegal orders. In response, Mr. Trump posted on his "Truth Social" account that the actions constituted "SEDITIOUS BEHAVIOR AT THE HIGHEST LEVEL" and that "Each of these traitors to our Country should be ARRESTED AND PUT ON TRIAL." Further he stated that the conduct was "punishable by DEATH" and followed up with posting a reader response which said "HANG THEM GEORGE WASHINGTON WOULD". (Washington Post, November 20 at 4:37 PM 2025)

These courageous men and women, who have been personally attacked and defamed by Mr. Trump for exercising their First Amendment rights, would be an excellent group of Plaintiffs/Petitioners to consult with legal counsel about bringing one of the first Breach of Oath/Contract lawsuits.

Similarly, the collective "Epstein Victims" should consult with counsel about a redress of grievances suit against Mr. Trump for breach of his Oath/Contract by his bad faith and dishonest cover-up of the Epstein files and his involvement with Mr. Epstein. Grounds would include Mr. Trump working with the Speaker of the House to keep the body out of session during a highly damaging government shutdown just to avoid a vote on the files' release.

Members of each of these groups, and other prospective plaintiff/petitioner groups, should also consider consulting with the Attorneys General from their home states as possible legal counsel or co-counsel for their lawsuits. Similarly, interested public interest organizations should look to Attorneys General as possible co-counsel.

Breach of Oath/Contract suits coming at Mr. Trump from a variety of regions and/or states by different groups of plaintiffs, with variable primary sets of breach issues joined by related supplemental claims showing compelling, cumulative breaches, will place Mr. Trump on the defense in ways he has never contemplated nor experienced and maximize the chances of achieving several court decisions ending his Presidential Employment Contract.

—November 21, 2025

Table of Authorities

Case

AFGE, AFL-CIO v. Trump,
139 F.4th 1020,1034(9th Cir. 2025) 33

Black Lives Matter D.C. v. United States,
775 F.Supp.3d 241 14

Burlington N. and Santa Fe Ry. Co. v. United States,
556 U.S. 599, 614-15(2009) 16

Carroll v. Trump, 49 F.4th 759 14

Charter Bank v. Francoeur,
2012-NMCA-078, 287 P.3d 333 (2012) 53

Cole v.Young, 351 U.S. 536, 559 (1956) 34

Cmty. For Creative Non-Violence v. Reid
490 U.S.730, 752 n.31(1989) 16

County of Santa Clara v. Astra USA, Inc.
540 F.3d 1094 (9th Cir. 2008) 16

Gill v. Moco Thermal Indus.
981 F.2d 858 (6th Cir. 1992) 15

Hometown Fin., Inc. v. United States
60 Fed. Ct. 513 23

In re Trump, 926 F.3d 360 (4th Cir. 2019) 47

Kelley v. S. Pac. Co., 419 U.S. 318, 324 (1974) 15

Learning Resources, Inc. v. Trump
No. 24-1287 (U.S. Nov. 5, 2025) 61

Lujan v. Defenders of Wildlife
504 U.S. 555, 560-61 (1992) 53

Pac. Gas & Elec. Co. v. United States
838 F.3d 341 (Fed. Cir. 2016) 53

Panama Refining Co. v. Ryan
293 U.S. 388, 433 (1935) 33

Sandhu v. Bd. of Admin
108 Cal. App. 5th 1048 (2025) 15, 54

Thole et al. v. U.S. Bank N.A. et al.
590 U.S. 538 (2020) 17
Trump v. United States
603 U.S. 593 642, 643(2024) 49
United States v. Wong Kim Ark
169 U.S. 649, 649 (1898) 20
Vernon v State of California
116 Cal. App. 4th 114 (2004) 15, 54
Wallach v. Eaton Corp.
837 F.3d 356 (3d Cir. 2016) 16
Yee v Jewell 228 F.Supp.3d 48 (2017)16 16
Youngstown Sheet and Tube Co. v. Sawyer
343 U.S. 570, 585 1952 33

Statutes
4 U.S.C. §4 100
17 U.S.C. §§ 101–1332 (2012) 16
18 U.S.C. § 3281 68
40 Okla. Stat. § 600.7 54
42 U.S.C. §§ 9601–9675 16
5 U.S.C. § 2105(a)(1)(A) (2018) 14
Cal. Bus. & Prof. Code § 17200 et.al.) 84
Kan. Stat. Ann. § 44-1707 54

Other Authorities
Cassius VI, Mass. Gazette, Dec. 21, 1787 45

Citizens for Responsibility & Ethics in Wash.,
CREW Statement on January 6th Pardons (Jan. 20, 2025),
https://www.citizensforethics.org/news/press-releases/crew-statement-on-january-6th-pardons 45

"Constitutional Remedies: In One Era and Out the Other" by Professor Richard Fallon. Harvard Law Review, Vol. 136, Issue 5, pp. 1300-1366 (March 2023)...... 11, 12

"The Supreme Court's Trump Enablers..." by Atty. Simon Lazarus. "Smart News" 9/24/25........... 26

Abraham Lincoln, The Gettysburg Address (1863)..... 3,4

Anita Krishna-kumar, The Common Law ...Backdrop, 136Harv.L.Rev. 608, 610 (2022).................................... 16

Andrew Kent, Ethan J. Leib & Jed Handelsman Shugerman, *Faithful Execution and Article II*, 132 Harv. L. Rev. 2111, 2116 (2019).................. 29-30, 44

Arthur L. Corbin, *Corbin On Contracts* §§1-13 14

Arthur L. Corbin, *Corbin on Contracts* § 984, 969 (One Volume ed. 1952) 37-38

Arthur L. Corbin, *Corbin on Contracts* § 776-777 (1952) 52

B. Meyler, *The President as Officer Not Sovereign: The Paradox of Proportionality*, 133 Harv. L. Rev. F. 89 (2020)...................................... 14

Cassandra Dahnke & Tomas Spath, What Is Civility?, Inst. for Civility, https://www.instituteforcivility.org/who-we-are/what-is-civility/ 106

Cong. Rsch. Serv., Modes of Constitutional Interpretation, R45129 (2018).. 63

David Schultz, *Voices - The key to checking Trump's lawlessness is to discipline his lawyers,* https://www.latimes.com/opinion/story/2025-11-05/states- disbar-trump-lawyers- 87

Gary Lucks, You Are Not Alone: Your Roadmap to Effective Political Action (2025).......................................56-57

Jennifer Frey, Civility and Democracy, The Thomas B. Fordham Inst. (2021), https://fordhaminstitute.org/national/commentary/civility-democracy-and-education. 4,5

John Yoo, Our Anticompetitive Patriotism, 39 U.C. Davis L. Rev. 1243 (2006) 24

Letter from Ranking Member Jamie Raskin and Judiciary Comm. Democrats to Att'y Gen. Pam Bondi, Deputy Att'y Gen. Todd Blanche, and Assoc. Att'y Gen. Stanley Woodward (Oct. 28, 2025), https://democrats-judiciary.house.gov/media-center/press-releases/judiciary-democrats-expand-probe-demand-doj-officials-reject-president-s-corrupt-demand-for-230-million-payout..41-42

Magna Carta 1215...30

Mark R. Wolf, Why I Am Resigning, The Atlantic, (Nov. 9, 2025), https://www.theatlantic.com/ideas/2025/11/federal-judge-resignation-trump/684845/ 21-22

Mark Twain, The Czar's Soliloquy, N. Am. Rev., Mar. 1905, 345...24

Michael S. Paulsen, *The Constitution of Necessity*, 79 Notre Dame L. Rev. 1257 (2004); https://scholarship.law.nd.edu/ndlr/vol79/iss4/3 10

Moore, T. *Want to end dark money in politics? Montana holds the key* | Opinion. USA Today. https://www.usatoday.com/story/opinion/2025/09/17/ supreme-court-citizens-united-campaign-finance-politics/86116869007/ 84

Tracking Project 2025, naacpldf.org 84

ProgressiveReform.org https://progressivereform.org .. 24

Project 2025.Observer, https://www.project2025 observer/ 18, 24

Restatement (First) of Contracts at 558–62 (Am. L. Inst. 1932) 17

Restatement (Second) of Contracts § 161 cmt. b (Am. Law Inst. 1981) 30

Restatement (Second) of Contracts § 161 cmt. f (Am. Law Inst. 1981) 30

Restatement (Second) of Contracts § 2 (Am. Law Inst. 1981 51

Restatement (Second) of Contracts § 205 (e) (Am. L. Inst. 1981) 35

Restatement (Second) of Contracts § 207, (Am. L. Inst. 1981) 36

Restatement (Second) of Contracts § 241 (Am. Law Inst. 1981) 14,23

Restatement (Second) of Contracts § 250 (Am. Law Inst. 1981) 37

Restatement (Second) of Contracts § 251(2) (Am. Law Inst. 1981) 37

Restatement (Second) of Contracts §§ 160–162, 164, 167 (Am. Law Inst. 1981) 31

Restatement (Second) of Contracts §§ 344–385 (Am. Law Inst. 1981) 34

Restatement (Second) of Torts) Section 433A(1)(b) 16

Restatement (Third) of Restitution and Unjust Enrichment § 37 (Am. L. Inst. 2011 35

Stephen Breyer, *Reading The Constitution: Why I Chose Pragmatism, Not Textualism*, Preface, xvii (2024) 12

The Documentary History Of The Ratification Of The Constitution, 500 (John P. Kaminski, et al. eds., 2009) 11

The Federalist No. 47 (James Madison) 61

Thomas Paine, *Common Sense; Addressed to the Inhabitants of America* (1776) 107

Trump Judges Face Threats, The Hill (July 31, 2025, 2:28 PM),https://thehill.com/regulation/court-battles/ 5430326 -trump-judges-face-threats/ 59

Constitutional Provisions
U.S. Const. art. II, § 1, cls.7-8............................ 14, 29, 41
U.S. Const. art II, §§1-4 50
U.S. Const. art II, § 3 29
U.S. Const. art. I, § 9.. 46
U.S. Const. art. II, § 1, cl. 7 46
U.S. Const. art. III, § 2, cl. 1.3.1 53
U.S. Const. amend 25 §21 40
U.S. Const. amend. 1 §45 100

APPENDIX A

UNITED STATES GOVERNORS
BLUE AND SWING STATES

ARIZONA
Gov. Katie Hobbs
Office of the Governor
1700 W. Washington St.
Phoenix, AZ 85007
602-542-4331
engage@az.gov and azgovernor.gov

CALIFORNIA
Gov. Gavin Newsom
1021 O Street, Suite 9000
Sacramento, CA 95814
(916) 445-2841
governor@governor.ca.gov
gavin.newsom@gov.ca.gov

COLORADO
Gov. Jared Polis
State Capitol Bldg
200 E. Colfax Ave., Rm. 136
Denver, CO 80203
303-866-2471
Governorpolis@state.co.us

CONNECTICUT
Gov. Ned Lamont
Office of the Governor, State Capitol
210 Capitol Avenue
Hartford, CT 06106
860-566-4840
ct.gov/Office-of-the-Governor/Contact/Email-Governor-Lamont
Twitter: @GovNedLamont

DELAWARE
Gov. Matthew S. Meyer
150 Martin Luther King Jr Blvd
South Dover, DE 19901
302-744-4101
meyer@delaware.gov

GEORGIA
Gov. Brian Kemp
State Capitol,
206 Washington Street, Su 203
Atlanta, GA 30334
404-656-1776
georgia.governor@gov.state.ga.us

HAWAII
The Honorable Josh Green
Governor, State of Hawai'i
Executive Chambers
State Capitol
415 South Beretania St.
Honolulu, Hawai'i 96813
Phone: (808) 586-0034
https://governor.hawaii.gov

ILLINOIS
Gov. JB Pritzker
Office of the Governor
401 S. Spring St.
Springfield, IL 62704
217-782-6830

MAINE
Gov. Janet Mills
1 State House Station
Augusta, ME 04333
207-287-3531
governor@maine.gov

MARYLAND
Gov. Wes Moore
100 State Circle
Annapolis, Maryland 21401-1925
410-974-3901
Wes.moore@maryland.gov
X - @wesmoore

MASSACHUSETTS
Gov. Maura Healey
Massachusetts State House,
24 Beacon St.
Office of the Governor,
Room 280
Boston, MA 02133
617-725-4005
@MassGovernor on Twitter
@MassGovernor on Instagram

MICHIGAN
Gov. Gretchen Witmer
State Capitol
P.O. Box 30013
Lansing, Michigan 48909
517-335-7858 (Constituent Services)
contactmichigan@state.mi.us

MINNESOTA
Gov. Tim Walz
130 State Capitol
75 Rev Dr. Martin Luther King Jr. Blvd.
St. Paul, MN 55155
651-201-3400
info@walzforgovernor.org

NEVADA
Gov. Joe Lombardo
State Capitol Building
101 N. Carson Street
Carson City, NV 89701
775-684-5670

NEW HAMPSHIRE
Gov. Kelly Ayotte
Office of the Governor
State House
107 North Main Street
Concord, NH 03301
603-271-2121
GovernorAyotte@governor.nh.gov

NEW JERSEY
Gov. Phil Murphy (current)
The State House
P.O. Box 001
Trenton, NJ 08625
609-292-6000

NEW JERSEY, cont.
Gov elect (01/20/2026):
Mikie Sherrill (U.S. Congresswoman
Washington DC Office
1427 Longworth HOB
Washington, DC 20515
Phone: (202) 225-5034
Fax: (202) 225-3186
Livingston District Office
357 S. Livingston Avenue
Suite 201
Livingston, NJ 07039
Phone: (973) 526-5668

NEW MEXICO
Gov. Michelle Lujan Grisham
490 Old Santa Fe Trail Room 400
Santa Fe, NM 87501
505-476-2200
gwhitehead1028@gmail.com

NEW YORK
Gov. Kathy Hochul
NYS State Capitol Building
Albany, NY 12224
518-474-8390

NORTH CAROLINA
Gov. Josh Stein
Office of the Governor
20301 Mail Service Center
Raleigh, NC 27699-0301
919-814-2000

OREGON
Gov. Tina Kotek
900 Court Street
Suite 254
Salem, OR 97301-4047
503-378-4582
https://www.oregon.gov/gov/pages/contact-us.aspx

PENNSYLVANIA
Gov. Josh Shapiro
501 North 3rd Street
508 Main Capitol Building
Harrisburg, PA 17120
717-787-2500
governor@pa.gov

RHODE ISLAND
Gov. Dan McKee
82 Smith Street
Providence, RI 02903
401-222-2080
governor@governor.ri.gov

VERMONT
Gov. Phil Scott
Office of the Governor
109 State Street, Pavilion
Montpelier, VT 05609
802-828-3333
phil.scott@gmail.com

VIRGINIA
Gov. Glenn Youngkin
Governor's Office
Patrick Henry Building, Third Floor.
Mailing Address
111 East Broad Street
Richmond, VA 23219.
804.786.2211
glenn.youngkin@governor.virginia.gov
Gov.Elect (1/20/2026)
US Congresswoman
Abigail D. Spanberger,
info@abigailspanberger.com,
804-223-0770
www.abigailspanberger.com,
PO Box 312
Glen Allen, VA, 23058-3121.

WASHINGTON
Gov. Bob Ferguson
Legislative Bldg
416 Sid Snyder Ave. SW,
Suite 200
P.O. Box 40002
Olympia, WA 98504-0002
360-902-4111
www.governor.wa.gov

WISCONSIN
P.O. Box 7863
Madison, WI 5370
608-266-1212
Tony.evers@wiconsin.gov.

APPENDIX B

STATE ATTORNEYS GENERAL
BLUE AND SWING STATES

ARIZONA
Attorney General Kris Mayes
Email: AGInfo@azag.gov
Address: 2005 N Central Avenue, Phoenix, AZ 85004
Phone: 602-542-5025

CALIFORNIA
Attorney General Rob Bonta
Email: DisabilityRights@doj.ca.gov
Address: Attorney General's Office,
California Department of Justice,
P.O. Box 944255
Sacramento, CA 94244-2550

COLORADO
Attorney General Philip Weiser
Email: Email Submission Form
Address: Office of the Attorney General
Colorado, Department of Law
Ralph L. Carr Judicial Building,
1300 Broadway, 10th Floor
Denver, CO 80203
Phone: 720-508-6000
https://complaints.coag.gov/s/contact-us

CONNECTICUT
Attorney General William Tong
Email: Attorney.General@ct.gov
Address: Office of the Attorney General,
165 Capitol Avenue
Hartford, CT 06106
Phone: 860-808-5318

DELAWARE
Attorney General Kathy Jennings
Carvel State Office Bldg.
820 N. French St.
Wilmington, DE 19801
302-577-8400

GEORGIA
Attorney General Chris Carr
Email: None listed
Address: 40 Capitol Square, SW
Atlanta, Georgia 30334
Phone: (404) 458-3600

HAWAII
Attorney General Anne E. Lopez
Email: Email Submission Form
Address: Department of the Attorney General,
425 Queen Street
Honolulu, HI 96813
Phone: 808-586-1500
https://ag.hawaii.gov/contact-us/email-the-department-of-ag/.

ILLINOIS
Attorney General
Kwame Raoul
Email: Email Submission Form
Address: Office of the Illinois Attorney General Constituent Services,
115 S. LaSalle Street
Chicago, Illinois 60603
Phone: 217-782-1090
https://forms.illinoisattorneygeneral.gov/Forms/OAG_ContactUs

MAINE
Attorney General
Aaron Frey
Email: attorney.general@maine.gov
Address: 6 State House Station,
Augusta, ME 04333
Phone: 207-626-8800

MARYLAND
Attorney Anthony G. Brown
Email: civilrights@oag.state.md.us
Email Submission Form
Address: 200 St. Paul Place
Baltimore, MD 21202
Phone: 410-576-6300

MASSACHUSETTS
Attorney General
Andrea Joy Campbell
Email: AGOcommunityengagement@state.ma.us
betany.h.brown@mass.gov
ADA Coordinator
Address: 1 Ashburton Place, 20th Floor,
Boston, MA 02108
Phone: 617-727-2200
617-963-2917

MICHIGAN
Attorney General
Dana Nessel
Email: miag@michigan.gov
Address: G. Mennen Williams Building,
525 W. Ottawa Street
P.O. Box 30212
Lansing, MI 48909
Phone: 517-335-7622

MINNESOTA
Attorney General
Keith Ellison
Email: None listed
Address: 445 Minnesota Street, Suite 600
St. Paul, MN 55101
Phone: 651-296-3353 (Twin Cities Calling Area)
800-657-3787 (Outside the Twin Cities)

NEVADA
Attorney General
Aaron D. Ford
Email: AgInfo@ag.nv.gov
Address: Office of the
Attorney General
100 North Carson Street
Carson City, NV 89701
Phone: 775-684-1100

NEW HAMPSHIRE
Attorney General
John Formella
Email: attorneygen-
eral@doj.nh.gov
Address: 1 Granite Place
South
Concord, NH 03301
Phone: 603-271-3658

NEW JERSEY
Attorney General
 Matthew J. Platkin
Email: Email Submission
Form
Address: Office of the
Attorney General
25 Market Street
PO Box 081 Trenton, NJ
08625-0081
Phone: 609-984-5828
https://www.njoag.gov/con-
tact/office-of-constituent-ser-
vices/

NEW MEXICO
Attorney General
Raúl Torrez
Email: Email Submission
Form (click on "form")
Address: 408 Galisteo Street
Villagra Building,
Santa Fe, NM 87501
Phone: 505-490-4060
https://nmdoj.gov/contact-us/

NEW YORK
Attorney General
Letitia James
Email: Email Submission
Form
Address: Office of the New
York State Attorney General
The Capitol,
Albany NY 12224-0341
Phone: 800-771-7755
https://ag.ny.gov/contact-ag

NORTH CAROLINA
Attorney General
Jeff Jackson
Email: Email Submission
Form (scroll down)
Address: 9001 Mail Service
Center
Raleigh, NC 27699-9001
Phone: 919-716-6400
919-716-0058 (En Espanol)
https://ncdoj.gov/contact-doj/

OREGON
Attorney General
Dan Rayfield
Email: AttorneyGeneral@doj.oregon.gov
Address: Oregon Department of Justice
1162 Court St
NE, Salem, OR 97301-4096
Phone: 503-378-4400

PENNSYLVANIA
Attorney General David W. Sunday, Jr.
Email: Email Submission Form
Address: Pennsylvania Office of Attorney General
Strawberry Square, Harrisburg, PA 17120
Phone: 717-787-3391
https://www.attorneygeneral.gov/contact/

RHODE ISLAND
Attorney General
Peter F. Neronha
Email: None listed
Address: Rhode Island Office of the Attorney General, 150 South Main Street, Providence, RI 02903
Phone: 401-274-4400

VERMONT
Attorney General
Charity R. Clark
ago.info@vermont.gov
Address: 109 State Street, Montpelier, VT 05609
Phone: 802-828-3171

VIRGINIA
Attorney General
Jason S. Miyares
Constituent Affairs Form
Address: Office of the Attorney General
202 North Ninth Street
Richmond, Virginia 23219
Phone: 804-786-2071
https://vaoag.my.site.com/OAG/s/constituent-affairs

WASHINGTON
Attorney General
Nick Brown
Email Contact Form
Address: 1125 Washington Street SE
PO Box 40100
Olympia, WA 98504-0100
Phone: 360-753-6200
https://fortress.wa.gov/atg/formhandler/ago/ContactForm.aspx

WISCONSIN
Attorney General Josh Kaul
Email Submission Form (Scroll down)
Address: Attorney General
PO Box 7857
Madison, WI 53707-7857
Phone: 608-266-1221
https://www.doj.state.wi.us/ag/contact

APPENDIX C

BLUE STATES AND SWING STATES

DISTRICT COURTS CHIEF JUDGES

US COURT OF APPEALS CHIEF JUDGES

UNITED STATES SUPREME COURT

DISTRICT COURTS
Chief Judges

ARIZONA
THE HONORABLE
JENNIFER G. ZIPPS,
CHIEF JUDGE
United States District Court
Evo A. DeConcini U.S. Courthouse
405 West Congress Street, Suite 5190
Tucson, AZ 85701-5053
Phone: (520) 205-4610

UNITED STATES DISTRICT COURT - DISTRICT OF ARIZONA
Sandra Day O'Connor U.S. Courthouse
401 West Washington Street
Phoenix, AZ 85003

CALIFORNIA
Central District
THE HONORABLE
DOLLY M. GEE,
CHIEF JUDGE
US Courthouse
350 West 1st Street
Los Angeles, CA 90012
DMG_Chambers@cacd.uscourts.gov.

Northern District of California:
THE HONORABLE
RICHARD G. SEEBORG,
CHIEF DISTRICT JUDGE
Peckham Federal Bldg.
280 S. First St.
San Jose, CA 95113
(408) 535-5357

Southern District of California:
THE HONORABLE
CYNTHIA ANN BASHANT
CHIEF JUDGE
Schwartz U.S. Courthouse
221 W. Broadway
San Diego, CA 92101
(619) 321-0256

Eastern District of California:
THE HONORABLE
TROY L. NUNLEY,
CHIEF JUDGE
U.S. Courthouse
501 I St.
Sacramento, CA 95814-2322
(916) 930-4163

COLORADO
THE HONORABLE
PHILLIP A. BRIMMER,
CHIEF JUDGE
Alfred A. Arraj U.S.
Courthouse
901 - 19th St., Rm. A641
Denver, CO 80294-3589
303) 335-2794

DELAWARE
THE HONORABLE
COLM F. CONNELLY,
CHIEF JUDGE
Boggs Fed. Bldg. (Lockbox 31)
844 King St., Rm. 2325
Wilmington, DE 19801
(302) 573-6310

GEORGIA
Northern District
THE HONORABLE
LEIGH M. MAY,
CHIEF JUDGE
2167 Russell Federal
Bldg.
75 Ted Turner Drive
Atlanta, GA 30303-3361
(404) 215-1510

Middle District
Leslie J. Abrams Gardner,
Chief Judge
C.B. King U.S.
Courthouse
201 West Broad Ave.
Albany, GA 31701
(229) 430-8432

Southern District
THE HONORABLE
R. STAN BAKER,
CHIEF JUDGE
125 Bull St., Rm 306
Savannah, GA 31401
(912) 650-4081

HAWAII
THE HONORABLE
DERRICK K. WATSON,
CHIEF JUDGE
U.S. Courthouse
300 Ala Moana Blvd.
Honolulu, HI 96850-0353
(808) 541-1300

ILLINOIS
Northern District
THE HONORABLE
VIRGINIA M.
KENDALL
CHIEF JUDGE
2378 Dirksen Bldg.
219 S. Dearborn St.
Chicago, IL 60604
(312) 435-5692

Central District
THE HONORABLE
SARA L. DARROW,
CHIEF JUDGE
48 U.S. Courthouse
211 19th St.
Rock Island, IL 61201
(309) 793-5779

Southern District
THE HONORABLE
NANCY J.
ROSENSTENGEL,
CHIEF JUDGE
Federal Courthouse
750 Missouri Ave.
East St. Louis, IL 62201
(618) 482-9172

MAINE
THE HONORABLE
ERIC M. STORMS,
ACTING
Gignoux U.S. Courthouse
156 Federal St.
Portland, ME 04101
(207) 780-3356

MARYLAND
THE HONORABLE
GEORGE L. RUSSELL
III, CHIEF JUDGE
101 W. Lombard St.
Baltimore, MD 21201
(410) 962-7880

MASSACHUSETTS
THE HONORABLE
DENISE J. CASPER,
CHIEF JUDGE
Moakley U.S. Courthouse
1 Courthouse Way
Boston, MA 02210
617) 748-9177

MICHIGAN
Eastern District
THE HONORABLE
STEPHEN J. MURPHY,
CHIEF JUDGE
Theodore Levin CtHse
231 W. Lafayette Blvd.
Detroit, MI 48226
(313) 234-2680

Western District
THE HONORABLE
HALA Y. JARBOU,
CHIEF JUDGE
128 Fed. Bldg. & U.S. CtHse
315 W. Allegan St.
Lansing, MI 48933
517) 853-7360

MINNESOTA
THE HONORABLE
PATRICK JOSEPH
SCHILTZ, CHIEF
JUDGE
Burger Federal Bldg.
316 N. Robert St.
St. Paul, MN 55101
(651) 848-1900

NEVADA
THE HONORABLE
ANDREW P. GORDON,
CHIEF JUDGE
Lloyd D. George U.S. CtHse
333 Las Vegas Blvd. South
Las Vegas, NV 89101
(702) 868-4940

NEW HAMPSHIRE
THE HONORABLE
LANDYA B.
McCAFFERTY,
CHIEF JUDGE
Rudman U.S. Courthouse
55 Pleasant St.
Concord, NH 03301
(603) 225-1423

NEW JERSEY
THE HONORABLE
RENEE MARIE BUMB,
CHIEF JUDGE
M.H. Cohen U.S. Courthouse
1 John F. Gerry Plaza
400 Cooper St.
Camden, NJ 08101
(856) 757-5020

NEW MEXICO
THE HONORABLE
KENNETH J.
GONZALES, CHIEF
JUDGE
U.S. District Court
100 N. Church St.
Las Cruces, NM 88001
(575) 528-1640

NEW YORK
Northern District
THE HONORABLE
BRENDA K. SANNES,
CHIEF JUDGE
James M. Hanley Fed. Bldg.
100 S. Clinton St.
Syracuse, NY 13261
(315) 234-8500

Eastern District
THE HONORABLE
MARGO KITSY
BRODIE, CHIEF JUDGE
U.S. Courthouse
225 Cadman Plaza East
Brooklyn, NY 11201
(718) 613-2145

Southern District
THE HONORABLE
LAURA TAYLOR
SWAIN, CHIEF JUDGE
U.S. Courthouse, Foley Sq.
New York, NY 10007-1581
(212) 805-0417

Western District
THE HONORABLE
ELIZABETH A.
WOLFORD,
CHIEF JUDGE
U.S. Courthouse
100 State St.
Rochester, NY 14614-1324
(585) 613-4320

NORTH CAROLINA
Eastern District
THE HONORABLE
RICHARD E. MYERS II,
CHIEF JUDGE
1003 S. 17th St.
Wilmington, NC 28401
(910) 815-4663

Middle District
THE HONORABLE
CATHERINE C.
EAGLES, CHIEF
JUDGE *(ON SENIOR STATUS)*
Preyer Federal CtHse
324 W. Market St., Rm. 401
Greensboro, NC 27401
(336) 332-6070

Western District
THE HONORABLE
MARTIN K.
REIDINGER,
CHIEF JUDGE
110 U.S. Courthouse
100 Otis St.
Asheville, NC 28801-2611
(828) 771-7260

OREGON
THE HONORABLE
MICHAEL J.
MCSHANE,
CHIEF JUDGE
5700 U.S. Courthouse
400 E. Eighth Ave.
Eugene OR 97401-2706
(541) 431-4150

PENNSYLVANIA
Eastern District
THE HONORABLE
WENDY
BEETLESTONE,
CHIEF JUDGE
4000 Byrne U.S. Courthouse
Independence Mall,
West 601 Market St.
Philadelphia, PA 19106-1797
(267) 299-7450

Middle District
THE HONORABLE
MATTHEW W. BRANN,
CHIEF JUDGE
Walter T. Schneebeli Fed. Bldg.
240 W. Third St., #218
Williamsport 17701
(570) 323-9772

Western District
THE HONORABLE
MARK RAYMOND
HORNAK,
CHIEF JUDGE
U.S. Post Office & CtHse
700 Grant St.
Pittsburgh, PA 15219
(412) 208-7433

RHODE ISLAND
THE HONORABLE
JOHN J. MCCONNELL
JR., CHIEF JUDGE
One Exchange Terrace
Providence, RI 02903
(401) 752-7200

VERMONT
THE HONORABLE
CHRISTINA REISS,
CHIEF JUDGE
Federal Building
P.O. Box 478
Burlington, VT 05402
(802) 773-2205

VIRGINIA
Eastern District
THE HONORABLE
MARK S. DAVIS,
CHIEF JUDGE
Hoffman U.S. CtHse
600 Granby St., Norfolk,
VA 23510-1811
(757) 222-7014

Western District
THE HONORABLE
ELIZABETH K.
DILLON, CHIEF JUDGE
242 Franklin Rd. S.W.
Roanoke, VA 24011
(540) 857-5120

WASHINGTON
Eastern District
THE HONORABLE
STANLEY A. BASTIAN,
CHIEF JUDGE
P.O. Box 2706 (98907-2706)
Wm. O. Douglas Bldg.
25 S. Third St.
Yakima, WA 98901
(509) 573-6600

Western District
THE HONORABLE
DAVID G. ESTUDILLO,
CHIEF JUDGE
3100 Union Station Bldg.
1717 Pacific Ave.
Tacoma, WA 98402-3226
(253) 882-3840

WISCONSIN
Eastern District
THE HONORABLE
PAMELA PEPPER,
CHIEF JUDGE
U.S. Courthouse
517 East Wisconsin Ave.
Milwaukee, WI 53202
414) 297-1596J.

Western District
THE HONORABLE
JAMES D. PETERSON,
CHIEF JUDGE
Kastenmeier U.S. CtHse
120 N. Henry St., Rm. 320
Madison, WI 53703
(608) 264-5156

UNITED STATES COURT OF APPEALS
Chief Judges

First Circuit Maine, Massachusetts, New Hampshire, Puerto Rico, Rhode Island
David J. Barron, Chief Judge
John J. Moakley U.S. CtHse
1 Courthouse Way
Boston, MA 02210
(617) 748-9008

Second Circuit Connecticut, New York, Vermont
Debra Ann Livingston, Chief Judge
Thurgood Marshall U.S. CtHse
40 Foley Sq.
New York, NY 10007
(212) 857-8500

Third Circuit Delaware, New Jersey, Pennsylvania, U.S. Virgin Islands
Michael A. Chagares, Chief Judge
21400 U.S. Courthouse
601 Market St.
Philadelphia, PA 19106-1790
(215) 597-2995

Fourth Circuit Maryland, North Carolina, South Carolina, Virginia, West Virginia
Albert Diaz, Chief Judge
Powell U.S. CtHse Annex
1100 E. Main St., Su 501
Richmond, VA 23219-3517
(704) 444-7790

Fifth Circuit Louisiana, Mississippi, Texas
Jennifer W. Elrod, Chief Judge
515 Rusk Ave.
Houston, TX 77002-2603
(713) 257-7590

Sixth Circuit Kentucky, Michigan, Ohio, Tennessee
Jeffrey S. Sutton, Chief Judge
540 Potter Stewart U.S. CtHse
100 E. Fifth St.
Cincinnati, OH 45202-3988
(513) 564-7000

Seventh Circuit Illinois, Indiana, Wisconsin
Michael B. Brennan, Chief Judge
Dirksen U.S. Courthouse
371 S. Dearborn St.
Chicago, IL 60604
(312) 435-5850

Eighth Circuit Arkansas, Iowa, Minnesota, Missouri, Nebraska, North Dakota, South Dakota
Steven M. Colloton, Chief Judge
461 U.S. Courthouse Anx
110 E. Court Ave.
Des Moines, IA 50309
(515) 284-6356

Ninth Circuit Alaska, Arizona, California, Hawaii, Idaho, Montana, Nevada, Oregon, Washington
Mary H. Murguia, Chief Judge
James R. Browning U.S. CtHse
95 Seventh St. (94103-1526)
P.O. Box 193939
San Francisco, CA 94119-3939
(415) 355-8000

Tenth Circuit Colorado, Kansas, New Mexico, Oklahoma, Utah, Wyoming
Jerome A. Holmes, Chief Judge
Byron White U.S. Courthouse
1823 Stout St.
Denver, CO 80257
(303) 844-3157

Eleventh Circuit Alabama, Florida, Georgia
William H. Pryor, Jr., Chief Judge
Tuttle Court of Appeals Bldg.
56 Forsyth St. N.W.
Atlanta, GA 30303-3147
(404) 335-6100

District of Columbia Circuit (1948-present)
Sri Srinivasan, Chief Judge
E. Barrett Prettyman CtHse
333 Constitution Ave. N.W.
Washington, DC 20001-2866
(202) 216-7080

UNITED STATES SUPREME COURT

U.S. Supreme Court
Supreme Court Bldg.
1 First St. NE
Washington, DC 20543
(202) 479-3000

Clerk: Scott Harris
(202) 479-3000 (switchboard)
(202) 479-3011 (clerk's office)
(202) 479-3211 (public information office)
(202) 479-3360 (opinion announcements)

Chief Justice
Roberts, John Glover, Jr. (2005-present)

Associate Justices
Alito, Samuel A., Jr. (2006-present)
Sotomayor, Sonia (2009-present)
Kagan, Elena (2010-present)
Gorsuch, Neil M. (2017-present)
Kavanaugh, Brett M. (2018-present)
Barrett, Amy Coney (2020-present)
Jackson, Ketanji Brown 2022-present

APPENDIX D

MAJOR VETERANS AND ACTIVE DUTY POLITICAL ADVOCACY ORGANIZATIONS

American Legion: The largest veterans' service organization, it advocates for service members, veterans, and their families.
The American Legion National Headquarters:
700 N. Pennsylvania St., P.O Box 1055,
Indianapolis, IN 46206
800.433.3318
https://www.votervoice.net/AmericanLegion/home
https://www.legion.org/advocacy/national-affairs
https://mylegion.org/PersonifyEbusiness/Donate#legion-org

AMVETS (American Veterans): A congressionally chartered veterans service organization that advocates for veterans' rights and helps veterans with career services and reintegration.
Family National Headquarters
265 North Ave.
Washington, PA 15301
AMVETS National Capital Headquarters.
4 Taft Court, Suite 350.
Rockville, MD 20850
https://www.amvets.org/advocacy
https://web.charityengine.net/amvets-support-us

Army Women's Foundation: Supports army women and veterans in their continued success, including through educational grants and scholarships, which can be a form of political support.
P.O. BOX 5030
Fort Lee, Virginia 23801
804-734-3078
info@awfdn.org
4310 Gregg Avenue Fort Lee,
Virginia 23801
https://awfdn.square.site

Common Defense: A veteran-led grassroots movement dedicated to protecting democracy and building a future where liberty and justice are for all, often through progressive action.
251 W 30th St #511
New York, NY 10001
https://commondefense.us/take-action/
https://commondefense.us/donate/
contact@commondefense.us

Disabled American Veterans (DAV): A nonpartisan organization that lobbies for legislation to improve the quality of life for veterans and their families.
810 Vermont Avenue NW,
Washington, D.C. 20420
https://mylegion.org/PersonifyEbusiness/Donate#legion-org
https://help.dav.org/page/66135/donate/

Iraq and Afghanistan Veterans of America (IAVA):
A post-9/11 veteran advocacy group known for its lobbying efforts and public awareness campaigns.
Paul Reickhoff, Executive Director
Paul@iava.org
80 M Street SE, Fl 2
WASHINGTON, DC 20003
(202) 544-7692
info@iava.org
https://iava.org/our-impact
https://iava.org/join-the-movement

Paralyzed Veterans of America: Lobbies on issues affecting paralyzed veterans and all people with disabilities.
1875 Eye St NW, Suite 1100,
Washington, DC 20006.
donations processing center
P.O. Box 758589,
Topeka, KS 66675-8589.
https://pva.org/research-resources/policy-priorities/
https://pva.org/research-resources/pva-action-force/
https://secure.pva.org/PVA/donate-pva?utm_source=website&utm_medium=web&utm_content=homepage_donate_topright&utm_campaign=evergreen

Semper Fi & America's Fund
825 College Blvd
Suite 102 • PMB 609
Oceanside, CA 92057
https://thefund.org/donate/
Phone: (760) 725-3680

Swords to Plowshares
401 Van Ness Avenue, Suite 313
San Francisco, CA 94102
https://www.swords-to-plowshares.org/resources/policy
https://www.swords-to-plowshares.org/donate#ways-to-give

Veterans of Foreign Wars (VFW): A nonpartisan organization that supports veterans and their families.
406 W 34th St,
Kansas City, MO 64111
(816) 756-3390
https://www.vfw.org/advocacy/grassroots-efforts
https://heroes.vfw.org/page/21776/donate/1?ea.tracking.id=vfwhomepage&utm_source=homepage&utm_medium=button

Veterans Campaign: A non-partisan organization that encourages, mentors, and prepares veterans for civic and political leadership as a "second service".
https://www.veteranscampaign.org/our-story
2024 Election Analysis
https://www.veteranscampaign.org/2024-election-analysis
https://www.veteranscampaign.org/donate

Veterans for American Ideals (VFAI): A project of Human Rights First, this coalition brings a bipartisan veterans' voice to human rights issues, U.S. policy, and confronting political extremism.
https://www.influencewatch.org/organization/veterans-for-american-ideals-vfai/

Vietnam Veterans of America (VVA): Focuses on a range of issues affecting Vietnam-era veterans, including healthcare and legal services.
719 Colesville Road, Suite 100,
Silver Spring, MD 20910
301-585-4000
https://vva.org/who-we-are/

VoteVets: A progressive PAC and action fund for veterans, military families, and their supporters. It runs independent spending campaigns to elect veterans to office at various levels and uses public campaigns to lift up veteran voices on national security and veterans' care issues.
VoteVets.org
PO Box 11293
Portland, OR 97211
https://votevets.org/doge-tipline
https://secure.actblue.com/contribute/page/vote_vets_pac?refcode=vv_webprimarynav
https://vva.org/donate/?form=FUN26MAIN&utm_source=main_donate

With Honor: Supports principled veterans across party lines who run for Congress and other elected offices
info@withhonor.org
700 Pennsylvania Avenue SE,
Washington, D.C. 20003

With Honor Action:
Works to pass critical legislation with bipartisan veteran lawmakers and supports the election of veterans who take the "With Honor Pledge".
https://withhonor.org/about/
https://withhonor.org/for-country-caucus/
https://withhonor.org/pledge/

Wounded Warriors
4899 Belfort Road Suite 300
Jacksonville, FL 32256
877.TEAM.WWP (832.6997)
https://www.woundedwarriorproject.org/programs/government-affairs

APPENDIX E

NON-PROFIT ORGANIZATIONS SUPPORTING AND/OR PURSUING LEGAL ACTION

Brennan Center for Justice at NYU School of Law: A nonpartisan institute focusing on voting rights, redistricting, and campaign finance reform.
   General Inquiries
   Ph 646.292.8310
   brennancenter@nyu.edu
   Donation Inquiries
   Alan Alejandro Prieto,
   Donor Services and Stewardship Manager
   Ph 646.925.8753
   donations@brennan.law.nyu.edu
   New York (Main Office)
   120 Broadway, Suite 1750
   New York, NY 10271
   Ph 646.292.8310
   brennancenter@nyu.edu
   Washington, D.C., Office
   777 6th St. NW, Suite 1100
   Washington, DC 20001
   Ph 202.249.7190

Common Cause: Advocates for pro-democracy reforms, including voting rights. Common Cause is a nonpartisan, 501(c)4 organization. Tax ID: 52-6078441. The Common Cause Education Fund is our 501(c)3 affiliate. Tax ID: 31-1705370.
https://www.commoncause.org/take-action/
https://www.commoncause.org/donate/

Democracy Docket
This is a non-profit entity, but it operates under the Hopewell Fund, a 501(c)(3) non-profit. It uses litigation to fight against suppressive voting laws and practices
sponsor@democracydocket.com
Democracy Docket Legal Fund:

Democracy Forward: Uses litigation to challenge anti-democratic actions.
https://democracyforward.org/get-involved/
https://democracyforward.org/action/donate/?source=top-nav

Indivisible Project: 501(c)(4) non-profit organization that engages in legislative advocacy and political campaigning.
PO Box 43884
Washington, DC 20010-0884
United States
Telephone: 301-778-8533
www.indivisible.org
>   **Indivisible Civics**: A 501(c)(3) charitable affiliate that focuses on public education and civic engagement, such as the Indivisible Truth Brigade program.
>   **Indivisible Action**: A hybrid political action committee (PAC) associated with the movement, which has an electoral program.

Issue One: A cross-partisan group working on campaign finance reform and election legitimacy.
https://issueone.org/about-us/
https://issueone.org/donate/

Lawyers' Committee for Civil Rights Under Law: Leads the nonpartisan **Election Protection** program.
https://www.lawyerscommittee.org/mission/
https://www.lawyerscommittee.org/mission/

League of Women Voters (LWV): A nonpartisan organization promoting informed participation, voter education, and voting rights advocacy.
https://donate.lwv.org/page/84107/donate/1

NAACP Legal Defense & Educational Fund: Uses courts to advocate for civil rights and protect voting access.
https://support.naacp.org/a/jointhefight/
https://naacp.org/donate

National Endowment for Democracy (NED): A private, nonprofit foundation dedicated to the growth and strengthening of democratic institutions around the world. **Protect Democracy**: Dedicated to preventing authoritarianism through litigation, education, and research.
(202) 378-9700
INFO@NED.ORG

Protect Democracy: We defend elections, the rule of law, and fact-based political debate against authoritarian threats — regardless of who wins or who is in power — and work to shape a better democracy for future generations.
https://protectdemocracy.org/authoritarian-threat-response/
https://protectdemocracy.org/donate/

Public Citizen: nonprofit consumer advocacy organization that champions the public interest in the halls of power. We defend democracy, resist corporate power, and fight to ensure that government works for the people – not big corporations. 22 current lawsuits against Trump Administration
https://www.citizen.org/act/
https://donate.citizen.org/page/59137/donate/1

State Democracy Defenders Fund
A nonpartisan, all-star team dedicated to stopping the assault on democracy and restoring American democracy.
https://www.democracydefendersfund.org/our-work
https://secure.actblue.com/donate/state-democracy-defenders-fund-2

APPENDIX F

US CONSTITUTION

DECLARATION OF INDEPENDENCE

THE UNITED STATES CONSTITUTION

We the People of the United States, in Order to form a more perfect Union, establish Justice, insure domestic Tranquility, provide for the common defence, promote the general Welfare, and secure the Blessings of Liberty to ourselves and our Posterity, do ordain and establish this Constitution for the United States of America.

Article I

Section 1: Congress
All legislative Powers herein granted shall be vested in a Congress of the United States, which shall consist of a Senate and House of Representatives.

Section 2: The House of Representatives
The House of Representatives shall be composed of Members chosen every second Year by the People of the several States, and the Electors in each State shall have the Qualifications requisite for Electors of the most numerous Branch of the State Legislature.

No Person shall be a Representative who shall not have attained to the Age of twenty five Years, and been seven Years a Citizen of the United States, and who shall not, when elected, be an Inhabitant of that State in which he shall be chosen.

Representatives and direct Taxes shall be apportioned among the several States which may be included within this Union, according to their respective Numbers, which shall be determined by adding to the whole Number of free Persons, including those bound to Service for a Term of Years, and excluding Indians not taxed, three fifths of all other Persons. he actual Enumeration shall be made within three Years after the first Meeting of the Congress of the United States, and within every subsequent Term of ten Years, in such Manner as they shall by Law direct.The Number of Representatives shall not exceed one for every thirty Thousand, but each State shall have at Least one Representative; and until such enumeration shall be made, the State of New Hampshire shall be entitled to chuse three, Massachusetts eight, Rhode-Island and Providence Plantations one, Connecticut five, New-York six, New Jersey four, Pennsylvania eight, Delaware one, Maryland six, Virginia ten, North Carolina five, South Carolina five, and Georgia three.

When vacancies happen in the Representation from any State, the Executive Authority thereof shall issue Writs of Election to fill such Vacancies.

The House of Representatives shall chuse their Speaker and other Officers;and shall have the sole Power of Impeachment.

Section 3: The Senate

The Senate of the United States shall be composed of two Senators from each State, chosen by the Legislature thereof, for six Years; and each Senator shall have one Vote. Immediately after they shall be assembled in Consequence of the first Election, they shall be divided as equally as may be into three Classes. The Seats of the Senators of the first Class shall be vacated at the Expiration of the second Year, of the second Class at the Expiration of the fourth Year, and of the third Class at the Expiration of the sixth Year, so that one third may be chosen every second Year; and if Vacancies happen by Resignation, or otherwise, during the Recess of the Legislature of any State, the Executive thereof may make temporary

Appointments until the next Meeting of the Legislature, which shall then fill such Vacancies.

No Person shall be a Senator who shall not have attained to the Age of thirty Years, and been nine Years a Citizen of the United States, and who shall not, when elected, be an Inhabitant of that State for which he shall be chosen.

The Vice President of the United States shall be President of the Senate, but shall have no Vote, unless they be equally divided.

The Senate shall chuse their other Officers, and also a President pro tempore, in the Absence of the Vice President, or when he shall exercise the Office of President of the United States.

The Senate shall have the sole Power to try all Impeachments. When sitting for that Purpose, they shall be on Oath or Affirmation. When the President of the United States is tried, the Chief Justice shall preside: And no Person shall be convicted without the Concurrence of two thirds of the Members present.

Judgment in Cases of Impeachment shall not extend further than to removal from Office, and disqualification to hold and enjoy any Office of honor, Trust or Profit under the United States: but the Party convicted shall nevertheless be liable and subject to Indictment, Trial, Judgment and Punishment, according to Law.

Section 4: Elections

The Times, Places and Manner of holding Elections for Senators and Representatives, shall be prescribed in each State by the Legislature thereof; but the Congress may at any time by Law make or alter such Regulations, except as to the Places of chusing Senators.

The Congress shall assemble at least once in every Year, and such Meeting shall be on the first Monday in December, unless they shall by Law appoint a different Day.

Section 5: Powers and Duties of Congress
Each House shall be the Judge of the Elections, Returns and Qualifications of its own Members,and a Majority of each shall constitute a Quorum to do Business; but a smaller Number may adjourn from day to day, and may be authorized to compel the Attendance of absent Members, in such Manner, and under such Penalties as each House may provide.

Each House may determine the Rules of its Proceedings, punish its Members for disorderly Behaviour, and, with the Concurrence of two thirds, expel a Member.

Each House shall keep a Journal of its Proceedings, and from time to time publish the same, excepting such Parts as may in their Judgment require Secrecy; and the Yeas and Nays of the Members of either House on any question shall, at the Desire of one fifth of those Present, be entered on the Journal.

Neither House, during the Session of Congress, shall, without the Consent of the other, adjourn for more than three days, nor to any other Place than that in which the two Houses shall be sitting.

Section 6: Rights and Disabilities of Members
The Senators and Representatives shall receive a Compensation for their Services, to be ascertained by Law, and paid out of the Treasury of the United States. They shall in all Cases, except Treason, Felony and Breach of the Peace, be privileged from Arrest during their Attendance at the Session of their respective Houses, and in going to

and returning from the same; and for any Speech or Debate in either House, they shall not be questioned in any other Place.

No Senator or Representative shall, during the Time for which he was elected, be appointed to any civil Office under the Authority of the United States, which shall have been created, or the Emoluments whereof shall have been encreased during such time; and no Person holding any Office under the United States, shall be a Member of either House during his Continuance in Office.

Section 7: Legislative Process

All Bills for raising Revenue shall originate in the House of Representatives; but the Senate may propose or concur with Amendments as on other Bills.

Every Bill which shall have passed the House of Representatives and the Senate, shall, before it become a Law, be presented to the President of the United States; If he approve he shall sign it, but if not he shall return it, with his Objections to that House in which it shall have originated, who shall enter the Objections at large on their Journal, and proceed to reconsider it. If after such Reconsideration two thirds of that House shall agree to pass the Bill, it shall be sent, together with the Objections, to the other House, by which it shall likewise be reconsidered, and if approved by two thirds of that House, it shall become a Law. But in all such Cases the Votes of both Houses shall be determined by yeas and Nays, and the Names of the Persons voting for and against the Bill shall be entered on the Journal of each House respectively. If any Bill shall not be returned by the President within ten Days (Sundays excepted) after it shall have been presented to him, the Same shall be a Law, in like Manner as if he had signed it, unless the Congress by their

Adjournment prevent its Return, in which Case it shall not be a Law.

Every Order, Resolution, or Vote to which the Concurrence of the Senate and House of Representatives may be necessary (except on a question of Adjournment) shall be presented to the President of the United States; and before the Same shall take Effect, shall be approved by him, or being disapproved by him, shall be repassed by two thirds of the Senate and House of Representatives, according to the Rules and Limitations prescribed in the Case of a Bill.

Section 8: Powers of Congress

The Congress shall have Power To lay and collect Taxes, Duties, Imposts and Excises, to pay the Debts and provide for the common Defence and general Welfare of the United States; but all Duties, Imposts and Excises shall be uniform throughout the United States;

To borrow Money on the credit of the United States;

To regulate Commerce with foreign Nations, and among the several States, and with the Indian Tribes;

To establish a uniform Rule of Naturalization, and uniform Laws on the subject of Bankruptcies throughout the United States;

To coin Money, regulate the Value thereof, and of foreign Coin, and fix the Standard of Weights and Measures;

To provide for the Punishment of counterfeiting the Securities and current Coin of the United States;

To establish Post Offices and post Roads;

To promote the Progress of Science and useful Arts, by securing for limited Times to Authors and Inventors the exclusive Right to their respective Writings and Discoveries;

To constitute Tribunals inferior to the supreme Court;

To define and punish Piracies and Felonies committed on the high Seas, and Offences against the Law of Nations;

To declare War, grant Letters of Marque and Reprisal, and make Rules concerning Captures on Land and Water;

To raise and support Armies, but no Appropriation of Money to that Use shall be for a longer Term than two Years;

To provide and maintain a Navy;

To make Rules for the Government and Regulation of the land and naval Forces;

To provide for calling forth the Militia to execute the Laws of the Union, suppress Insurrections and repel Invasions;

To provide for organizing, arming, and disciplining, the Militia, and for governing such Part of them as may be employed in the Service of the United States, reserving to the States respectively, the Appointment of the Officers, and the Authority of training the Militia according to the discipline prescribed by Congress;

To exercise exclusive Legislation in all Cases whatsoever, over such District (not exceeding ten Miles square) as may, by Cession of particular States, and the Acceptance of Congress, become the Seat of the Government of the United States, and to exercise like Authority over all Places purchased by the Consent of the Legislature of the State in which the Same shall be, for the Erection of Forts, Magazines, Arsenals, dock-Yards and other needful Buildings;-And

To make all Laws which shall be necessary and proper for carrying into Execution the foregoing Powers, and all other Powers vested by this Constitution in the

Government of the United States, or in any Department or Officer thereof.

Section 9: Powers Denied Congress
The Migration or Importation of such Persons as any of the States now existing shall think proper to admit, shall not be prohibited by the Congress prior to the Year one thousand eight hundred and eight, but a Tax or duty may be imposed on such Importation, not exceeding ten dollars for each Person.

The Privilege of the Writ of Habeas Corpus shall not be suspended, unless when in Cases of Rebellion or Invasion the public Safety may require it.

No Bill of Attainder or ex post facto Law shall be passed.

No Capitation, or other direct, Tax shall be laid, unless in Proportion to the Census or enumeration herein before directed to be taken.No Tax or Duty shall be laid on Articles exported from any State.

No Preference shall be given by any Regulation of Commerce or Revenue to the Ports of one State over those of another: nor shall Vessels bound to, or from, one State, be obliged to enter, clear, or pay Duties in another.

No Money shall be drawn from the Treasury, but in Consequence of Appropriations made by Law; and a regular Statement and Account of the Receipts and Expenditures of all public Money shall be published from time to time. No Title of Nobility shall be granted by the United States: And no Person holding any Office of Profit or Trust under them, shall, without the Consent of the Congress, accept of any present, Emolument, Office, or Title, of any kind whatever, from any King, Prince, or foreign State.

Section 10: Powers Denied to the States

No State shall enter into any Treaty, Alliance, or Confederation; grant Letters of Marque and Reprisal; coin Money; emit Bills of Credit; make any Thing but gold and silver Coin a Tender in Payment of Debts; pass any Bill of Attainder, ex post facto Law, or Law impairing the Obligation of Contracts, or grant any Title of Nobility.

No State shall, without the Consent of the Congress, lay any Imposts or Duties on Imports or Exports, except what may be absolutely necessary for executing it's inspection Laws: and the net Produce of all Duties and Imposts, laid by any State on Imports or Exports, shall be for the Use of the Treasury of the United States; and all such Laws shall be subject to the Revision and Controul of the Congress.

No State shall, without the Consent of Congress, lay any Duty of Tonnage, keep Troops, or Ships of War in time of Peace, enter into any Agreement or Compact with another State, or with a foreign Power, or engage in War, unless actually invaded, or in such imminent Danger as will not admit of delay.

Article II

Section 1

The executive Power shall be vested in a President of the United States of America.

He shall hold his Office during the Term of four Years, and, together with the Vice President, chosen for the same Term, be elected, as follows:

Each State shall appoint, in such Manner as the Legislature thereof may direct, a Number of Electors, equal to the whole Number of Senators and Representatives to which the State may be entitled in the Congress: but no

Senator or Representative, or Person holding an Office of Trust or Profit under the United States, shall be appointed an Elector.

The Electors shall meet in their respective States, and vote by Ballot for two Persons, of whom one at least shall not be an Inhabitant of the same State with themselves. And they shall make a List of all the Persons voted for, and of the Number of Votes for each; which List they shall sign and certify, and transmit sealed to the Seat of the Government of the United States, directed to the President of the Senate. The President of the Senate shall, in the Presence of the Senate and House of Representatives, open all the Certificates, and the Votes shall then be counted. The Person having the greatest Number of Votes shall be the President, if such Number be a Majority of the whole Number of Electors appointed; and if there be more than one who have such Majority, and have an equal Number of Votes, then the House of Representatives shall immediately chuse by Ballot one of them for President; and if no Person have a Majority, then from the five highest on the List the said House shall in like Manner chuse the President. But in chusing the President, the Votes shall be taken by States, the Representation from each State having one Vote; A quorum for this Purpose shall consist of a Member or Members from two thirds of the States, and a Majority of all the States shall be necessary to a Choice. In every Case, after the Choice of the President, the Person having the greatest Number of Votes of the Electors shall be the Vice President. But if there should remain two or more who have equal Votes, the Senate shall chuse from them by Ballot the Vice President.

The Congress may determine the Time of chusing the Electors, and the Day on which they shall give their

Votes; which Day shall be the same throughout the United States.

No Person except a natural born Citizen, or a Citizen of the United States, at the time of the Adoption of this Constitution, shall be eligible to the Office of President; neither shall any Person be eligible to that Office who shall not have attained to the Age of thirty five Years, and been fourteen Years a Resident within the United States. In Case of the Removal of the President from Office, or of his Death, Resignation, or Inability to discharge the Powers and Duties of the said Office, the Same shall devolve on the Vice President, and the Congress may by Law provide for the Case of Removal, Death, Resignation or Inability, both of the President and Vice President, declaring what Officer shall then act as President, and such Officer shall act accordingly, until the Disability be removed, or a President shall be elected.

The President shall, at stated Times, receive for his Services, a Compensation, which shall neither be encreased nor diminished during the Period for which he shall have been elected, and he shall not receive within that Period any other Emolument from the United States, or any of them.

Before he enter on the Execution of his Office, he shall take the following Oath or Affirmation:--"I do solemnly swear (or affirm) that I will faithfully execute the Office of President of the United States, and will to the best of my Ability, preserve, protect and defend the Constitution of the United States."

Section 2
The President shall be Commander in Chief of the Army and Navy of the United States, and of the Militia of the several States, when called into the actual Service of the

United States; he may require the Opinion, in writing, of the principal Officer in each of the executive Departments, upon any Subject relating to the Duties of their respective Offices, and he shall have Power to grant Reprieves and Pardons for Offences against the United States, except in Cases of Impeachment.

He shall have Power, by and with the Advice and Consent of the Senate, to make Treaties, provided two thirds of the Senators present concur; and he shall nominate, and by and with the Advice and Consent of the Senate, shall appoint Ambassadors, other public Ministers and Consuls, Judges of the supreme Court, and all other Officers of the United States, whose Appointments are not herein otherwise provided for, and which shall be established by Law: but the Congress may by Law vest the Appointment of such inferior Officers, as they think proper, in the President alone, in the Courts of Law, or in the Heads of Departments.

The President shall have Power to fill up all Vacancies that may happen during the Recess of the Senate, by granting Commissions which shall expire at the End of their next Session.

Section 3

He shall from time to time give to the Congress Information of the State of the Union, and recommend to their Consideration such Measures as he shall judge necessary and expedient; he may, on extraordinary Occasions, convene both Houses, or either of them, and in Case of Disagreement between them, with Respect to the Time of Adjournment, he may adjourn them to such Time as he shall think proper; he shall receive Ambassadors and other public Ministers; he shall take Care that the Laws be faithfully executed, and shall Commission all the Officers of the United States.

Section 4
The President, Vice President and all civil Officers of the United States, shall be removed from Office on Impeachment for, and Conviction of, Treason, Bribery, or other high Crimes and Misdemeanors.

Article III

Section 1
The judicial Power of the United States, shall be vested in one supreme Court, and in such inferior Courts as the Congress may from time to time ordain and establish. The Judges, both of the supreme and inferior Courts, shall hold their Offices during good Behaviour, and shall, at stated Times, receive for their Services, a Compensation, which shall not be diminished during their Continuance in Office.

Section 2
The judicial Power shall extend to all Cases, in Law and Equity, arising under this Constitution, the Laws of the United States, and Treaties made, or which shall be made, under their Authority;--to all Cases affecting Ambassadors, other public Ministers and Consuls;--to all Cases of admiralty and maritime Jurisdiction;--to Controversies to which the United States shall be a Party;--to Controversies between two or more States;--between a State and Citizens of another State;--between Citizens of different States;--between Citizens of the same State claiming Lands under Grants of different States, and between a

State, or the Citizens thereof, and foreign States, Citizens or Subjects.

In all Cases affecting Ambassadors, other public Ministers and Consuls, and those in which a State shall be Party, the supreme Court shall have original Jurisdiction. In all the other Cases before mentioned, the supreme Court shall have appellate Jurisdiction, both as to Law and Fact, with such Exceptions, and under such Regulations as the Congress shall make.

The Trial of all Crimes, except in Cases of Impeachment; shall be by Jury; and such Trial shall be held in the State where the said Crimes shall have been committed; but when not committed within any State, the Trial shall be at such Place or Places as the Congress may by Law have directed.

Section 3
Treason against the United States, shall consist only in levying War against them, or in adhering to their Enemies, giving them Aid and Comfort. No Person shall be convicted of Treason unless on the Testimony of two Witnesses to the same overt Act, or on Confession in open Court.

The Congress shall have Power to declare the Punishment of Treason, but no Attainder of Treason shall work Corruption of Blood, or Forfeiture except during the Life of the Person attainted.

Article IV

Section 1
Full Faith and Credit shall be given in each State to the public Acts, Records, and judicial Proceedings of every other State. And the Congress may by general Laws

prescribe the Manner in which such Acts, Records and Proceedings shall be proved, and the Effect thereof.

Section 2
The Citizens of each State shall be entitled to all Privileges and Immunities of Citizens in the several States.

A Person charged in any State with Treason, Felony, or other Crime, who shall flee from Justice, and be found in another State, shall on Demand of the executive Authority of the State from which he fled, be delivered up, to be removed to the State having Jurisdiction of the Crime.

No Person held to Service or Labour in one State, under the Laws thereof, escaping into another, shall, in Consequence of any Law or Regulation therein, be discharged from such Service or Labour, but shall be delivered up on Claim of the Party to whom such Service or Labour may be due.

Section 3
New States may be admitted by the Congress into this Union; but no new State shall be formed or erected within the Jurisdiction of any other State; nor any State be formed by the Junction of two or more States, or Parts of States, without the Consent of the Legislatures of the States concerned as well as of the Congress.

The Congress shall have Power to dispose of and make all needful Rules and Regulations respecting the Territory or other Property belonging to the United States; and nothing in this Constitution shall be so construed as to Prejudice any Claims of the United States, or of any particular State.

Section 4

The United States shall guarantee to every State in this Union a Republican Form of Government, and shall protect each of them against Invasion; and on Application of the Legislature, or of the Executive (when the Legislature cannot be convened) against domestic Violence.

Article V

The Congress, whenever two thirds of both Houses shall deem it necessary, shall propose Amendments to this Constitution, or, on the Application of the Legislatures of two thirds of the several States, shall call a Convention for proposing Amendments, which, in either Case, shall be valid to all Intents and Purposes, as Part of this Constitution, when ratified by the Legislatures of three fourths of the several States, or by Conventions in three fourths thereof, as the one or the other Mode of Ratification may be proposed by the Congress; Provided that no Amendment which may be made prior to the Year One thousand eight hundred and eight shall in any Manner affect the first and fourth Clauses in the Ninth Section of the first Article; and that no State, without its Consent, shall be deprived of its equal Suffrage in the Senate.

Article VI

All Debts contracted and Engagements entered into, before the Adoption of this Constitution, shall be as valid against the United States under this Constitution, as under the Confederation.

This Constitution, and the Laws of the United States which shall be made in Pursuance thereof; and all Treaties made, or which shall be made, under the Authority of the

United States, shall be the supreme Law of the Land; and the Judges in every State shall be bound thereby, any Thing in the Constitution or Laws of any State to the Contrary notwithstanding.

The Senators and Representatives before mentioned, and the Members of the several State Legislatures, and all executive and judicial Officers, both of the United States and of the several States, shall be bound by Oath or Affirmation, to support this Constitution; but no religious Test shall ever be required as a Qualification to any Office or public Trust under the United States.

Article VII

The Ratification of the Conventions of nine States, shall be sufficient for the Establishment of this Constitution between the States so ratifying the Same.

First Amendment
Congress shall make no law respecting an establishment of religion, or prohibiting the free exercise thereof; or abridging the freedom of speech, or of the press; or the right of the people peaceably to assemble, and to petition the Government for a redress of grievances.

Second Amendment
A well regulated Militia, being necessary to the security of a free State, the right of the people to keep and bear Arms, shall not be infringed.

Third Amendment
No Soldier shall, in time of peace be quartered in any house, without the consent of the Owner, nor in time of war, but in a manner to be prescribed by law.

Fourth Amendment

The right of the people to be secure in their persons, houses, papers, and effects, against unreasonable searches and seizures, shall not be violated, and no Warrants shall issue, but upon probable cause, supported by Oath or affirmation, and particularly describing the place to be searched, and the persons or things to be seized.

Fifth Amendment

No person shall be held to answer for a capital, or otherwise infamous crime, unless on a presentment or indictment of a Grand Jury, except in cases arising in the land or naval forces, or in the Militia, when in actual service in time of War or public danger; nor shall any person be subject for the same offence to be twice put in jeopardy of life or limb; nor shall be compelled in any criminal case to be a witness against himself, nor be deprived of life, liberty, or property, without due process of law; nor shall private property be taken for public use, without just compensation.

Sixth Amendment

In all criminal prosecutions, the accused shall enjoy the right to a speedy and public trial, by an impartial jury of the State and district wherein the crime shall have been committed, which district shall have been previously ascertained by law, and to be informed of the nature and cause of the accusation; to be confronted with the witnesses against him; to have compulsory process for obtaining witnesses in his favor, and to have the Assistance of Counsel for his defence.

Seventh Amendment
In Suits at common law, where the value in controversy shall exceed twenty dollars, the right of trial by jury shall be preserved, and no fact tried by a jury, shall be otherwise re-examined in any Court of the United States, than according to the rules of the common law.

Eighth Amendment
Excessive bail shall not be required, nor excessive fines imposed, nor cruel and unusual punishments inflicted.

Ninth Amendment
The enumeration in the Constitution, of certain rights, shall not be construed to deny or disparage others retained by the people.

10th Amendment
The powers not delegated to the United States by the Constitution, nor prohibited by it to the States, are reserved to the States respectively, or to the people.

11th Amendment
The Judicial power of the United States shall not be construed to extend to any suit in law or equity, commenced or prosecuted against one of the United States by Citizens of another State, or by Citizens or Subjects of any Foreign State.

12th Amendment
The Electors shall meet in their respective states and vote by ballot for President and Vice-President, one of whom, at least, shall not be an inhabitant of the same state with themselves; they shall name in their ballots the person voted for as President, and in distinct ballots the person

voted for as Vice-President, and they shall make distinct lists of all persons voted for as President, and of all persons voted for as Vice-President, and of the number of votes for each, which lists they shall sign and certify, and transmit sealed to the seat of the government of the United States, directed to the President of the Senate; -- the President of the Senate shall, in the presence of the Senate and House of Representatives, open all the certificates and the votes shall then be counted; -- The person having the greatest number of votes for President, shall be the President, if such number be a majority of the whole number of Electors appointed; and if no person have such majority, then from the persons having the highest numbers not exceeding three on the list of those voted for as President, the House of Representatives shall choose immediately, by ballot, the President. But in choosing the President, the votes shall be taken by states, the representation from each state having one vote; a quorum for this purpose shall consist of a member or members from two-thirds of the states, and a majority of all the states shall be necessary to a choice. And if the House of Representatives shall not choose a President whenever the right of choice shall devolve upon them, before the fourth day of March next following, then the Vice-President shall act as President, as in the case of the death or other constitutional disability of the President.-- The person having the greatest number of votes as Vice-President, shall be the Vice-President, if such number be a majority of the whole number of Electors appointed, and if no person have a majority, then from the two highest numbers on the list, the Senate shall choose the Vice-President; a quorum for the purpose shall consist of two-thirds of the whole number of Senators, and a majority of the whole number shall be necessary to a choice. But no person constitutionally ineligible to the office of President shall be eligible to that of Vice-President of the United States.

13th Amendment
Section 1
Neither slavery nor involuntary servitude, except as a punishment for crime whereof the party shall have been duly convicted, shall exist within the United States, or any place subject to their jurisdiction.

Section 2
Congress shall have power to enforce this article by appropriate legislation.

14th Amendment
Section 1
All persons born or naturalized in the United States, and subject to the jurisdiction thereof, are citizens of the United States and of the State wherein they reside. No State shall make or enforce any law which shall abridge the privileges or immunities of citizens of the United States; nor shall any State deprive any person of life, liberty, or property, without due process of law; nor deny to any person within its jurisdiction the equal protection of the laws.

Section 2
Representatives shall be apportioned among the several States according to their respective numbers, counting the whole number of persons in each State, excluding Indians not taxed. But when the right to vote at any election for the choice of electors for President and Vice-President of the United States, Representatives in Congress, the Executive and Judicial officers of a State, or the members of

the Legislature thereof, is denied to any of the male inhabitants of such State, being twenty-one years of age, and citizens of the United States or in any way abridged, except for participation in rebellion, or other crime, the basis of representation therein shall be reduced in the proportion which the number of such male citizens shall bear to the whole number of male citizens twenty-one years of age in such State.

Section 3

No person shall be a Senator or Representative in Congress, or elector of President and Vice-President, or hold any office, civil or military, under the United States, or under any State, who, having previously taken an oath, as a member of Congress, or as an officer of the United States, or as a member of any State legislature, or as an executive or judicial officer of any State, to support the Constitution of the United States, shall have engaged in insurrection or rebellion against the same, or given aid or comfort to the enemies thereof. But Congress may by a vote of two-thirds of each House, remove such disability.

Section 4

The validity of the public debt of the United States, authorized by law, including debts incurred for payment of pensions and bounties for services in suppressing insurrection or rebellion, shall not be questioned. But neither the United States nor any State shall assume or pay any debt or obligation incurred in aid of insurrection or rebellion against the United States, or any claim for the loss or emancipation of any slave; but all such debts, obligations and claims shall be held illegal and void.

Section 5
The Congress shall have power to enforce, by appropriate legislation, the provisions of this article.

15th Amendment
Section 1
The right of citizens of the United States to vote shall not be denied or abridged by the United States or by any State on account of race, color, or previous condition of servitude.

Section 2
The Congress shall have power to enforce this article by appropriate legislation.

16th Amendment
The Congress shall have power to lay and collect taxes on incomes, from whatever source derived, without apportionment among the several States, and without regard to any census or enumeration.

17th Amendment
The Senate of the United States shall be composed of two Senators from each State, elected by the people thereof, for six years; and each Senator shall have one vote. The electors in each State shall have the qualifications requisite for electors of the most numerous branch of the State legislatures.

When vacancies happen in the representation of any State in the Senate, the executive authority of such State shall issue writs of election to fill such vacancies: Provided, That the legislature of any State may empower the executive thereof to make temporary appointments until the people fill the vacancies by election as the legislature may direct.

This amendment shall not be so construed as to affect the election or term of any Senator chosen before it becomes valid as part of the Constitution.

18th Amendment
Section 1
After one year from the ratification of this article the manufacture, sale, or transportation of intoxicating liquors within, the importation thereof into, or the exportation thereof from the United States and all territory subject to the jurisdiction thereof for beverage purposes is hereby prohibited.

Section 2
The Congress and the several States shall have concurrent power to enforce this article by appropriate legislation.

Section 3
This article shall be inoperative unless it shall have been ratified as an amendment to the Constitution by the legislatures of the several States, as provided in the Constitution, within seven years from the date of the submission hereof to the States by the Congress.

19th Amendment
The right of citizens of the United States to vote shall not be denied or abridged by the United States or by any State on account of sex. Congress shall have power to enforce this article by appropriate legislation.

20th Amendment
Section 1
The terms of the President and the Vice President shall end at noon on the 20th day of January, and the terms of Senators and Representatives at noon on the 3d day of January, of the years in which such terms would have ended if this article had not been ratified; and the terms of their successors shall then begin.

Section 2
The Congress shall assemble at least once in every year, and such meeting shall begin at noon on the 3rd day of January, unless they shall by law appoint a different day.

Section 3
If, at the time fixed for the beginning of the term of the President, the President elect shall have died, the Vice President elect shall become President. If a President shall not have been chosen before the time fixed for the beginning of his term, or if the President elect shall have failed to qualify, then the Vice President elect shall act as President until a President shall have qualified; and the Congress may by law provide for the case wherein neither a President elect nor a Vice President elect shall have qualified, declaring who shall then act as President, or the manner in which one who is to act shall be selected, and such person shall act accordingly until a President or Vice President shall have qualified.

Section 4
The Congress may by law provide for the case of the death of any of the persons from whom the House of Representatives may choose a President whenever the right of choice shall have devolved upon them, and for the case of

the death of any of the persons from whom the Senate may choose a Vice President whenever the right of choice shall have devolved upon them.

Section 5
Sections 1 and 2 shall take effect on the 15th day of October following the ratification of this article.

Section 6
This article shall be inoperative unless it shall have been ratified as an amendment to the Constitution by the legislatures of three-fourths of the several States within seven years from the date of its submission.

21st Amendment
Section 1
The eighteenth article of amendment to the Constitution of the United States is hereby repealed.

Section 2
The transportation or importation into any State, Territory, or possession of the United States for delivery or use therein of intoxicating liquors, in violation of the laws thereof, is hereby prohibited.

Section 3
This article shall be inoperative unless it shall have been ratified as an amendment to the Constitution by conventions in the several States, as provided in the Constitution, within seven years from the date of the submission hereof to the States by the Congress.

22nd Amendment
Section 1
No person shall be elected to the office of the President more than twice, and no person who has held the office of President, or acted as President, for more than two years of a term to which some other person was elected President shall be elected to the office of the President more than once. But this Article shall not apply to any person holding the office of President when this Article was proposed by the Congress, and shall not prevent any person who may be holding the office of President, or acting as President, during the term within which this Article becomes operative from holding the office of President or acting as President during the remainder of such term.

Section 2
This article shall be inoperative unless it shall have been ratified as an amendment to the Constitution by the legislatures of three-fourths of the several States within seven years from the date of its submission to the States by the Congress.

23rd Amendment
Section 1
The District constituting the seat of Government of the United States shall appoint in such manner as Congress may direct.

A number of electors of President and Vice President equal to the whole number of Senators and Representatives in Congress to which the District would be entitled if it were a State, but in no event more than the least populous State; they shall be in addition to those appointed by the States, but they shall be considered, for the purposes of the election of President and Vice President, to be electors appointed by a State; and they shall meet in the District and perform such duties as provided by the twelfth article of amendment.

Section 2
The Congress shall have power to enforce this article by appropriate legislation.

24th Amendment
Section 1
The right of citizens of the United States to vote in any primary or other election for President or Vice President, for electors for President or Vice President, or for Senator or Representative in Congress, shall not be denied or abridged by the United States or any State by reason of failure to pay poll tax or other tax.

Section 2
The Congress shall have power to enforce this article by appropriate legislation.

25th Amendment
Section 1
In case of the removal of the President from office or of his death or resignation, the Vice President shall become President.

Section 2
Whenever there is a vacancy in the office of the Vice President, the President shall nominate a Vice President who shall take office upon confirmation by a majority vote of both Houses of Congress.

Section 3

Whenever the President transmits to the President pro tempore of the Senate and the Speaker of the House of Representatives his written declaration that he is unable to discharge the powers and duties of his office, and until he transmits to them a written declaration to the contrary, such powers and duties shall be discharged by the Vice President as Acting President.

Section 4

Whenever the Vice President and a majority of either the principal officers of the executive departments or of such other body as Congress may by law provide, transmit to the President pro tempore of the Senate and the Speaker of the House of Representatives their written declaration that the President is unable to discharge the powers and duties of his office, the Vice President shall immediately assume the powers and duties of the office as Acting President. Thereafter, when the President transmits to the President pro tempore of the Senate and the Speaker of the House of Representatives his written declaration that no inability exists, he shall resume the powers and duties of his office unless the Vice President and a majority of either the principal officers of the executive department or of such other body as Congress may by law provide, transmit within four days to the President pro tempore of the Senate and the Speaker of the House of Representatives their written declaration that the President is unable to discharge the powers and duties of his office. Thereupon Congress shall decide the issue, assembling within forty-eight hours for that purpose if not in session. If the Congress, within twenty-one days after receipt of the latter written declaration, or, if Congress is not in session, within twenty-one days after Congress is required to assemble, determines by two-thirds vote of both Houses that the President is unable to discharge the powers and duties of his office, the Vice President shall continue to discharge the same as Acting President; otherwise, the President shall resume the powers and duties of his office.

26th Amendment
Section 1
The right of citizens of the United States, who are eighteen years of age or older, to vote shall not be denied or abridged by the United States or by any State on account of age.

Section 2
The Congress shall have power to enforce this article by appropriate legislation.

27th Amendment
No law, varying the compensation for the services of the Senators and Representatives, shall take effect, until an election of Representatives shall have intervened.

DECLARATION OF INDEPENDENCE

In Congress, July 4, 1776
The unanimous Declaration of the thirteen united States of America, When in the Course of human events, it becomes necessary for one people to dissolve the political bands which have connected them with another, and to assume among the powers of the earth, the separate and equal station to which the Laws of Nature and of Nature's God entitle them, a decent respect to the opinions of mankind requires that they should declare the causes which impel them to the separation.

We hold these truths to be self-evident, that all men are created equal, that they are endowed by their Creator with certain unalienable Rights, that among these are Life, Liberty and the pursuit of Happiness.--That to secure these rights, Governments are instituted among Men, deriving their just powers from the consent of the governed, --That whenever any Form of Government becomes destructive of these ends, it is the Right of the People to alter or to abolish it, and to institute new Government, laying its foundation on such principles and organizing its powers in such form, as to them shall seem most likely to effect their Safety and Happiness. Prudence, indeed, will dictate that Governments long established should not be changed for light and transient causes; and accordingly all experience hath shewn, that mankind are more disposed to suffer, while evils are sufferable, than to right themselves by abolishing the forms to which they are accustomed. But when a long train of abuses and usurpations, pursuing invariably the same Object evinces a design to reduce them under absolute Despotism, it is their right, it is their duty, to throw off such Government, and to provide new Guards for their future security.--Such has been the patient sufferance of these Colonies; and such is now the necessity which constrains them to alter their former Systems of Government. The history of the present King of Great Britain is a history of repeated injuries and usurpations, all having in direct object the establishment of an absolute Tyranny over these States. To prove this, let Facts be submitted to a candid world.

He has refused his Assent to Laws, the most wholesome and necessary for the public good.

He has forbidden his Governors to pass Laws of immediate and pressing importance, unless suspended in their operation till his Assent should be obtained; and when so suspended, he has utterly neglected to attend to them.

He has refused to pass other Laws for the accommodation of large districts of people, unless those people would relinquish the right of Representation in the Legislature, a right inestimable to them and formidable to tyrants only.

He has called together legislative bodies at places unusual, uncomfortable, and distant from the depository of their public Records, for the sole purpose of fatiguing them into compliance with his measures.

He has dissolved Representative Houses repeatedly, for opposing with manly firmness his invasions on the rights of the people.

He has refused for a long time, after such dissolutions, to cause others to be elected; whereby the Legislative powers, incapable of Annihilation, have returned to the People at large for their exercise; the State remaining in the mean time exposed to all the dangers of invasion from without, and convulsions within.

He has endeavoured to prevent the population of these States; for that purpose obstructing the Laws for

Naturalization of Foreigners; refusing to pass others to encourage their migrations hither, and raising the conditions of new Appropriations of Lands.

He has obstructed the Administration of Justice, by refusing his Assent to Laws for establishing Judiciary powers.

He has made Judges dependent on his Will alone, for the tenure of their offices, and the amount and payment of their salaries.

He has erected a multitude of New Offices, and sent hither swarms of Officers to harrass our people, and eat out their substance.

He has kept among us, in times of peace, Standing Armies without the Consent of our legislatures.

He has affected to render the Military independent of and superior to the Civil power.

He has combined with others to subject us to a jurisdiction foreign to our constitution, and unacknowledged by our laws; giving his Assent to their Acts of pretended Legislation:

For Quartering large bodies of armed troops among us:

For protecting them, by a mock Trial, from punishment for any Murders which they should commit on the Inhabitants of these States:

For cutting off our Trade with all parts of the world:

For imposing Taxes on us without our Consent:

For depriving us in many cases, of the benefits of Trial by Jury:

For transporting us beyond Seas to be tried for pretended offences:

For abolishing the free System of English Laws in a neighbouring Province, establishing therein an Arbitrary government, and enlarging its Boundaries so as to render it at once an example and fit instrument for introducing the same absolute rule into these Colonies:

For taking away our Charters, abolishing our most valuable Laws, and altering fundamentally the Forms of our Governments:

For suspending our own Legislatures, and declaring themselves invested with power to legislate for us in all cases whatsoever.

He has abdicated Government here, by declaring us out of his Protection and waging War against us.

He has plundered our seas, ravaged our Coasts, burnt our towns, and destroyed the lives of our people.

He is at this time transporting large Armies of foreign Mercenaries to compleat the works of death, desolation and tyranny, already begun with circumstances of Cruelty & perfidy scarcely paralleled in the most barbarous ages, and totally unworthy the Head of a civilized nation.

He has constrained our fellow Citizens taken Captive on the high Seas to bear Arms against their Country, to become the executioners of their friends and Brethren, or to fall themselves by their Hands.

He has excited domestic insurrections amongst us, and has endeavoured to bring on the inhabitants of our frontiers, the merciless Indian Savages, whose known rule of warfare, is an undistinguished destruction of all ages, sexes and conditions.

In every stage of these Oppressions We have Petitioned for Redress in the most humble terms: Our repeated Petitions have been answered only by repeated injury. A Prince, whose character is thus marked by every act which may define a Tyrant, is unfit to be the ruler of a free people.

Nor have We been wanting in attentions to our Brittish brethren. We have warned them from time to time of attempts by their legislature to extend an unwarrantable jurisdiction over us. We have reminded them of the circumstances of our emigration and settlement here. We have appealed to their native justice and magnanimity, and we have conjured them by the ties of our common kindred to disavow these usurpations, which, would inevitably interrupt our connections and correspondence. They too have been deaf to the voice of justice and of consanguinity. We must, therefore, acquiesce in the necessity, which denounces our Separation, and hold them, as we hold the rest of mankind, Enemies in War, in Peace Friends.

We, therefore, the Representatives of the united States of America, in General Congress, Assembled, appealing to the Supreme Judge of the world for the rectitude of our intentions, do, in the Name, and by Authority of the good People of these Colonies, solemnly publish and declare, That these United Colonies are, and of Right ought to be Free and Independent States; that they are Absolved from all Allegiance to the British Crown, and that all political connection between them and the State of Great Britain, is and ought to be totally dissolved; and that as Free and Independent States, they have full Power to levy War, conclude Peace, contract Alliances, establish Commerce, and to do all other Acts and Things which Independent States may of right do. And for the support of this Declaration, with a firm reliance on the protection of divine Providence, we mutually pledge to each other our Lives, our Fortunes and our sacred Honor.

Georgia
Button Gwinnett
Lyman Hall
George Walton

North Carolina
William Hooper
Joseph Hewes
John Penn

South Carolina
Edward Rutledge
Thomas Heyward, Jr.
Thomas Lynch, Jr.
Arthur Middleton

Massachusetts
John Hancock

Maryland
Samuel Chase
William Paca
Thomas Stone
Charles Carroll of Carrollton

Virginia
George Wythe
Richard Henry Lee
Thomas Jefferson
Benjamin Harrison
Thomas Nelson, Jr.
Francis Lightfoot Lee
Carter Braxton

Pennsylvania
Robert Morris
Benjamin Rush
Benjamin Franklin
John Morton
George Clymer
James Smith
George Taylor
James Wilson
George Ross

Delaware
Caesar Rodney
George Read
Thomas McKean

New York
William Floyd
Philip Livingston
Francis Lewis
Lewis Morris

New Jersey
Richard Stockton
John Witherspoon
Francis Hopkinson
John Hart
Abraham Clark

New Hampshire
Josiah Bartlett
William Whipple

Massachusetts
Samuel Adams
John Adams
Robert Treat Paine
Elbridge Gerry

Rhode Island
Stephen Hopkins
William Ellery

Connecticut
Roger Sherman
Samuel Huntington
William Williams
Oliver Wolcot

Acknowledgments

From the moment Donald Trump was declared the winner of the November 2024 Presidential Election, I could not stop thinking about the prospect of watching him take the Presidential Oath of Office on January 20, 2025. I was certain that he would be lying.

Thus began a several-month brainstorming period during which I searched for a legal pathway to end Mr. Trump's predictable lawless Presidency. Early on, I began to focus on the contractual nature of the Oath of Office and would talk with colleagues about remedies for breaches. A few were immediately dismissive, noting they had never heard of the ideas or that there was nothing expressly in the Constitution to support my strategy. Most would quickly pronounce that there was no way to convince a majority on the Supreme Court to rule against Mr. Trump, so why bother?

And then there were my other legal friends, including Gary Lucks and Doug Carstens, who were very supportive from the beginning. Their continuing encouragement has been invaluable.

When I introduced the idea of the book to Carmen Berry and Carolyn Rafferty, the principals at the Writers Integrity Network (WIN), they were very excited and have been quite patient while waiting for the manuscript. I am very thankful for the opportunity to work with two passionate and highly gifted professionals.

Along the way, I was in touch with Winston Hickox and Professor Oliver Houck, who were supportive but reserved judgment until they read the final work product. Happily, you see their names in the endorsement section of this book, and I am most thankful for their very positive comments.

My non-lawyer friends Don Miller and Chuck Warner have been hearing about the project almost weekly, and their evolving perspectives and related questions have been invaluable to my attempt to write for a broader, non-legal audience.

I want to thank my cousins, Claire Harrison and Gerald Shoaf, for their enthusiastic support, and my friends, Carole H. Kuck and Sabrina Davidson, for their collaboration on the "Oath Peace Symbol" design. Thanks also to Jon Elliott for his careful review of the manuscript, to Eric Schnurer for his comments on the central legal strategy, and to Jenee Berry and Dylan Lucks for their work on the Appendices.

My Editor, Valeri Mills Barnes, has amazed me with her rock-solid attention to detail and her enthusiasm for the subject matter. I am grateful for her most excellent work.

Finally, without Gary Luck's inspiration, dedication, and relentless support, this book and the book series would not have come to fruition.

About the Author

Kevin Johnson holds a bachelor's degree in government from the University of Redlands (1975), a master's degree in political science from Rutgers University (1976), and a Juris Doctorate from the University of California at Davis (1980). He worked as a Contracts Teaching Assistant for two years while in law school.

From 1976 to 1977, Johnson engaged in international travel and studies that significantly impacted his professional trajectory towards working against abuses of government power. He attended graduate school classes at Punjab University, in the city of Chandigarh in Northern India studying the impact of religious traditions on Indian politics. When he first arrived, Indians had been living under a National Emergency declared a year earlier by Prime Minister Indira Gandhi.

The Emergency allowed censorship of the press, suspension of civil liberties, arrests of political opponents and a consolidation of power without judicial oversight. An ongoing National Family Planning Program forced sterilizations on approximately 8.1 million young Indian men and women. In rural villages, there were instances where police arrived unannounced in buses at dawn, grabbed young people at random and took them to be sterilized without any form of due process.

As a then Rotary Club International Scholar, Johnson had an opportunity, along with another American graduate student, to visit privately with the Prime Minister. When asked what message she would like conveyed to Rotary Clubs in the United States, she calmly said: "Tell the United States to stay out of our business."

On the way home from India, Johnson visited Tehran that was ruled at the time by the Shah of Iran, a dictator installed through a U.S.-supported coup. After Iran, Johnson worked as a volunteer on a "kibbutz" in Israel, on the Mediterranean Sea, near the Gaza Strip. Armed guards patrolled the "kibbutz" 24 hours a day as there was a constant threat of terrorist attacks. It was very unsettling being around people every day with Uzi machine guns casually strapped over their shoulders.

Upon returning home, he pursued his law degree at Martin Luther King Jr. Hall, at U.C. Davis, California. He has been a member of the California State Bar since 1980 and is an experienced civil trial and appellate lawyer. He holds the prestigious Martindale-Hubbell Preeminent Attorney rating of "AV," reflecting the highest level of legal ability and ethics as rated by legal peers and the judiciary. Fewer than five percent of attorneys nationwide have the equivalent standing.

Johnson is also admitted to practice in the Central and Southern U.S. District Courts in California and before the U.S. Ninth Circuit Court of Appeals. He has negotiated with and/or litigated against major oil companies, national insurance carriers, regional and local governments, the State of California, and the U.S. Government.

He has represented Fortune 500 Companies, routinely guided litigation clients into and through mediations, is credentialed as a mediator, and has assisted as a mediator and/or moderator in a variety of settings and jurisdictions.

Johnson has served on a variety of non-profit boards since the mid-1980s and was active in nationwide "Get Out the Vote" efforts during the 2008, 2012, 2020, and 2024 presidential elections.

In 2008 and 2012, he worked as a volunteer lawyer in a "Voter Protection" capacity during early voting at the Downtown Registrar's Office in Cleveland, Ohio, answering voter questions and helping ensure that everyone legally qualified could vote. In 2012, he observed firsthand how newly adopted state election laws sought to suppress the black vote in Cleveland by drastically limiting, compared to 2008, the days and hours available for early voting.

Additional, prior experiences with government abuse included working for the U.S. House of Representatives in 1975 and investigating Nixon Administration manipulation of the federal civil service through planned, "constructive terminations" of career civil servants to create job openings for political supporters.

Johnson has observed a wide range of individual conflicts and government abuses over the course of his career and continues to work to resolve disputes whenever possible. Success however depends upon people being willing to talk to each other, to make agreements in good faith and to keep their word. Where circumstances, personalities and/or priorities make this impossible, it's time for the parties to part ways and move on with their lives.

www.ingramcontent.com/pod-product-compliance
Lightning Source LLC
Chambersburg PA
CBHW070623030426
42337CB00020B/3896